Tahiti
and French Polynesia

Claude Hervé-Bazin

J·P·M
PUBLICATIONS

Contents

This Way Tahiti	**3**
Flashback	**7**
On the Scene	**15**
Tahiti	*15*
Tahiti's Sister Isles	*25*
Tuamotu and Gambier Islands	*42*
Austral Islands	*48*
Marquesas Islands	*51*
Cultural Notes	**64**
Shopping	**67**
Dining Out	**69**
Sports	**72**
The Hard Facts	**74**
Index	80

Map

Papeete	17

Fold-out maps

French Polynesia

This Way Tahiti

Paradise on Earth

The word "Tahiti" has a special magic, conjuring up an image of exotic delights and sensual pleasure. It has done so ever since the Age of Enlightenment in the 18th century, an era steeped in romanticism and the birth of new ideas. Europe dreamed of the "noble savage", handsome, generous, peace-loving and happily ignorant of "civilization" in his own Garden of Eden. The first to promote this idea was the French navigator, Bougainville. Tahiti—and the rest of Polynesia—has enchanted generations of explorers and writers from Captain Cook to Herman Melville, Jack London and Robert Louis Stevenson, and inspired artists such as Gauguin. Many a mariner, relaxing in this fabulous archipelago after months spent at sea, has been dazzled by the charms of the island girls or *vahines*.

The splendid scenery does little to dispel the image of paradise on earth. Scored by valleys and crowned by razor-sharp peaks, the islands rise majestically above translucent lagoons ringed by coral *motus*. Once taboo because they were believed to be inhabited by malevolent spirits, these isles offer beaches of virgin sands fringed with screwpines and coconut palms. The sultry air and warm rain, the cool waterfalls, the exuberant vegetation, the flowers of brilliant colours and heady fragrance, all conspire to create an atmosphere of glorious beauty.

How It All Began

Guided by the faint glow of the stars and drawing on their intimate knowledge of nature, the Polynesians conquered a new world—a stretch of ocean as wide as a continent. No other people has ever colonized the seas across such vast distances, but the memory of their achievement has not survived the generations. Instead, myths evolved to satisfy the people's need to understand their past. The ancient beliefs have largely disappeared today, but legends recurring all through the archipelago recount the history of the islands, beginning with their creation.

To the ancient Polynesians, the cradle of the earth and their religious centre was Havai'i, now known as Raiatea. An enormous earth-fish, drifting off the southwest coast of Havai'i, broke into pieces, giving birth to the Society Islands. The tale might have

ended there, but in this land of exclusively oral tradition, the pride and rivalry of the chiefs have generated a tangled web of contradictory stories.

Bora Bora, originally named Mai Te Pora, meaning "created by the gods", set the cat among the pigeons by claiming to have been drawn out of the ocean by the creator god Ta'aroa, the Unique One, before all the other islands. Except, of course, Raiatea. At least, that is what they say on Bora Bora. One thing is sure: it was from there that the seven sacred canoes left to colonize the far reaches of the "Polynesian Triangle", a region more water than land, with its three tips at Hawaii to the north, New Zealand to the southwest and Easter Island to the southeast.

The Marquesas have another version of events, the same as is told on Hawaii. The god Maui, a great angler, caught the islands on the end of his fishing line and hauled them up from the depths of the ocean.

A Geology Lesson

A map of the South Pacific looks something like a vast expanse of sky spangled with constellations of islands. French Polynesia—the

In the Marquesas, dances maintain a link with the past.

word is derived from the Greek *poly* (many) and *nesos* (island)—comprises exactly 118, all produced by volcanic activity at the end of the tertiary era. At a depth of 4,000 m (13,000 ft) on the ocean floor, lava welled through cracks in the earth's crust, known as "hot spots". With each new eruption, the lava piled up higher, eventually rising above the surface. An island was born. Gradually, with the movement of the continental plates and heaving subterranean thrusts, other submarine volcanoes were formed, creating a chain. Some of them grew slowly into islands, others never emerged above the waves.

The same process was repeated over and over again: the wind brought seeds which grew into plants, then birds and other animals colonized the new land. Rings of coral built up around the rim. Meanwhile, erosion was already shaping the islands as hurricane-force winds and rain and, above all, the pounding waves lashed against their flanks.

All the Polynesian islands were created in this way, though the larger and more recent isles, such as Tahiti, have been less affected by erosion. But other, smaller islands like Huahine and Bora Bora are already disintegrating. They are all destined to disappear over time—but only to be reincarnated. For the coral is progressively building up around them, forming a ring of life. Sediment is deposited and *motus* (coral islands) are formed; in due course vegetation takes root. The Tuamotu atolls, barely breaking the surface of the ocean, are perfect examples of this process—they are the vestiges of ancient "high islands", whittled away by time and the elements then submerged by the waves. In the place of a former volcano, there is now a lagoon.

The People

Despite a turbulent history, the Polynesians, *Maohi* in their own language, have lost nothing of their sense of enjoyment. Every dawn heralds the birth of a new day to be lived to the full. Who needs to worry? Food can easily be picked from the trees or fished from the lagoon. The simple life, warm welcome and generosity of the people are not just legends. The first sailors to reach these shores made that happy discovery. Items may have mysteriously disappeared from the ships, but why should they complain, when the vahines offered their charms in such an uninhibited way?

Several generations later, the outcome is a population of kaleidoscopic variety. It is estimated that barely 15 per cent of French Polynesia's 220,000 inhabitants are of pure Maohi blood. Half of these are under 20 years of age. This is scarcely surprising, for children have always been sacred in Polynesian eyes. The so-called "demis", officially of mixed race, also account for 15 per cent, while Europeans make up 12 per cent and Asians 4 per cent. The Asian community forms a commercially active minority, and few are the islands where the small shops are not run by a *Tinito* (Chinese) shopkeeper. The remainder of the population is of diverse and often mixed origin. One thing is clear from this human cocktail—in Polynesia, racism has simply no place.

The Church is one of the two pillars of Polynesian society, the other being the family. Missionaries fervently spread the Word, and the region today is 54 per cent Protestant and 30 per cent Catholic, with the rest adhering for the most part to various American sects.

At one time Polynesia almost became British. It has remained French, but today's young generation is dreaming of a cultural rebirth. The Tahitians, in particular, are now reclaiming their language and their heritage. In the 1960s, traditional dances were revived, and tattooing is back in fashion. The most adventurous set out to rediscover the Pacific aboard great canoes similar to those of their ancestors.

flashback

Ancestors

It was once thought that the population of Polynesia originally came from America or even some "lost continent". However, the truth has been ascertained without any doubt: archaeological, ethnological and linguistic studies all confirm that the elements of Polynesian life began in South-East Asia.

At the end of the last Ice Age, peoples from the island of Borneo, taking advantage of the drop in sea level, crossed the narrows separating them from Sahul, a vast expanse of land comprising New Guinea, New Zealand and Australia. Communities were established as far as the Solomon Islands. There, expansion came to a temporary halt, for no land could be seen beyond.

Much later, probably between 1500 and 1000 BC, mariners developed viable techniques of construction and navigation on the high seas, and were thus able to venture further. They gradually colonized an immense territory, reaching Vanuatu, Fiji, Tonga and Samoa aboard great double canoes fitted with sails.

Probably driven into exile by a demographic explosion, their descendants landed on the Marquesas a thousand years later. From there, they colonized Hawaii in the 6th century, and, three hundred years later, the Society Islands and Easter Island, then the Gambier Islands and New Zealand in about AD 1000. Two-thirds of the Pacific Ocean came under the control of a single people, covering a triangular area with its points at Hawaii in the north, New Zealand in the southwest and Easter Island in the southeast.

Dynasties were established in the Society Islands and the Marquesas, generally extending their power over a very limited territory. Inter-tribal warfare was frequent. Society was hierarchical, dominated by an aristocracy (the *ari'i*) from whom were drawn the chiefs and priests. Human sacrifice was exacted for worship of the gods, and carried out at the *marae* (sanctuary). Raiatea in the Society Islands came to prominence as the seat of power and centre of religious activity.

First Contacts

In 1521, the Portuguese navigator Magellan rounded Cape Horn, becoming the first European to enter the Pacific. He sailed close to the Tuamotu, landed on Puka

FLASHBACK

The Arahurahu marae, one of the many ancient Maohi religious sites.

Puka and reached Guam after a voyage of 99 days. He was killed in a skirmish in the Philippines, but the financial success of the expedition, which returned with a cargo of spices from the Moluccas, was enough to encourage other navigators to follow in his wake. The legend of a *Terra Australis Incognita* (the future Australia) goaded them on.

In 1595, the Spaniard Alvaro de Mendana reached the island of Hiva Oa. He gallantly named his new-found archipelago the Marquesas, after the Marchioness de Mendoza, wife of his commanding officer, the viceroy of Peru. When the islanders came out to meet them, the Spanish found them too bold and opened fire. The death toll is variously given as between 70 and 200, depending on the source. The Portuguese Fernandez de Queiros arrived in turn on the Marquesas and continued from there to another island he called Sagittaria. It may have been Tahiti, but the records have been lost. From their anchorages in the Philippines and Mexico, the Spanish established their control over commercial traffic in the North Pacific. In 1620, the Dutchman Jacob Roggeveen cruised around the Tuamotu and disembarked at Rangiroa, calling it the Isle of Flies.

FLASHBACK

Despite these early discoveries, it was really the French and English who undertook the exploration of Polynesia.

The Noble Savage

In June 1767, *H.M.S. Dolphin*, under the command of Captain Samuel Wallis of the Royal Navy, dropped anchor in Matavai Bay, five days after sighting Tahiti. The islanders welcomed him warmly. Wallis raised the Union Jack and named the island King George III. He recorded that there was an abundance of the three items essential to any sailor —water, pigs and women.

Bartering proved a great success. Nails were most appreciated by the Tahitians who appeared to be unfamiliar with metal. However, Wallis was soon obliged to put a stop to this trade, as the *Dolphin*'s crew, enthusiastically seeking to pay the favours of the local ladies, started to wrench bits of metal off the boat. Skirmishes broke out and Wallis was forced to fire the cannons to restore order.

Ten months later, Louis Antoine de Bougainville, the first Frenchman to circumnavigate the globe, disembarked from his ship the *Boudeuse*. Canoes swarmed around from all directions, laden with islanders waving banana leaves as a sign of welcome. Bougainville, a cultivated man and something of a poet, familiar with the romantic ideas of his time, was convinced that he had discovered the only corner of the world inhabited by people free of vice, without prejudices, without needs and without dissension. He wrote that Tahitians were devoted only to rest and sensual pleasures, and that they worshipped only Venus. Later, the ship's surgeon, Vivès, stated in the same vein that the delights tasted in Tahiti, the beauty and the availability of carnal pleasures, caused them to call the island *Nouvelle Cythère*, after the goddess of love. After nine days, Bougainville weighed anchor, leaving buried in the sand a document proclaiming French sovereignty. He took with him a young Tahitian named Aoturu, and on their return to France, Bougainville and several of his companions published accounts of the voyage. South Pacific fever swept Europe.

The Royal Geographical Society of London sent an expedition, led by Captain James Cook, with the mission to observe the impending transit of Venus across the sun, to explore the region and determine whether it was reasonable to suppose the existence of a continent or a vast unknown land. On board the *Endeavour* were the young naturalist Joseph Banks and various scientists, astronomers and artists. Cook arrived on Tahiti in 1769 and stayed there three months, naming the archipelago the Society Islands. When he left, he took on board a mariner named Tupia, who guided him as far as Raiatea, his native island, then to New Zealand and the eastern coast of Australia. Its mission accomplished, the *Endeavour* returned to England. Captain Cook returned twice more to the Pacific, landing again in Tahiti, then in the Marquesas in 1774, and finally returning to Hawaii where he was tragically killed in 1778. Cook was the first European to realise the importance of the links uniting the various groups of Polynesian peoples across the Pacific.

A few years later, in 1788, one of the most famous episodes in Pacific history took place. The *Bounty*, commanded by William Bligh, a former lieutenant of Captain Cook, was sent to Polynesia to carry breadfruit to the West Indies, where it was intended to grow them as food for the plantation slaves. Bligh and his crew spent 23 weeks in Tahiti. Shortly after casting off, the sailors, ill-treated by Bligh and not too keen on leaving the island, mutinied under the leadership of Fletcher Christian, the mate. The captain and 18 members of the crew were set adrift in a lifeboat. After several months, their voyage ended at Timor, some 6,500 km (4,000 miles) away, where the tides eventually washed them ashore. The *Bounty* and its mutinous crew reached the Austral Islands, then returned to Tahiti where they took aboard a dozen women and six men and set sail to look for a safe haven. They finally settled on Pitcairn, a small isolated isle more than 2,400 km (1,500 miles) southeast of Tahiti. Sixteen sailors who stayed behind on Tahiti were taken by the English ship *Pandora* in 1791. They were brought back to London for trial and duly hanged. Fletcher Christian was killed by his Tahitian companions.

End of the Gods

On his second voyage, Captain Cook began to notice the first ravages wrought by the arrival of Europeans. Diseases unknown in the region before then (influenza, chickenpox, syphilis) spread like wildfire. Merchant vessels and whalers started to call in regularly, making matters worse. In 1769, Tahiti's population numbered 35,000; within 30 years it was reduced to 8,000. By 1830, Tahiti and the Marquesas had become regular landfalls for whaling ships. The villages provided sanctuary for many a mutineer, deserter and escaped prisoner.

Meanwhile, 1797 marked the arrival—in the bay of Matavai—of Protestant missionaries sent out by the London Missionary Society. Initially, they met with little success. However, when the king of Tahiti, Pomare II, began looking for political allies to consolidate his power over the Society Islands, he converted to Christianity in 1812. This began the movement which would ultimately lead to the disappearance of traditional religion. The Tahitians felt abandoned by their own gods, who had provided no protection against disease or invasion, and gradually they turned towards the god of the foreigners. But the eternal rivalry between the French and the English was rekindled as the chiefs debated which of the two Christian gods —Protestant or Catholic—was the right one. Less active proselytizers, the French never caught up on the lead established by the Protestant missionaries.

After some hesitation, the rest of the Polynesian aristocracy followed the example of the Tahitian monarch. The missionaries, thus encouraged, attacked the pagan cults. Most of the *maraes* and *tikis* were destroyed, and the "missionary dress" was imposed on the women. By 1822, every island had a mission.

French Oceania

In 1836, Queen Pomare IV, at the instigation of Pastor Pritchard, expelled the French Catholic missionaries. In 1842, unable to convince Queen Victoria to take the archipelago under her protection, Queen Pomare was forced to accept the French protectorate after the intervention of Admiral Dupetit-Thouars. But French supremacy was not so easy to establish. Some of the island chiefs rebelled; Huahine and Raiatea resisted. By 1864, slave traders were deporting Marquesas islanders to the mines and plantations of South America. The following year saw the start of Asian immigration.

Pomare IV was succeeded by her son, Pomare V, an alcoholic and an ineffectual ruler. Crippled by debt, he abdicated in 1880 in favour of the French in exchange for a monthly pension of 5,000 francs. Five years later, the island and its neighbouring archipelagos became French Oceania (*Etablissements Français de l'Océanie*, E.F.O.). But Raiatea had still not surrendered, and it was only in February 1897 that the rebel chief Teraupo was finally captured. In 1903, when the Marquesas joined the colony, Polynesia became totally French.

Atomic Age

During World War I, the German battleships *Scharhorst* and *Gneisenau* launched raids against Tahiti from Nuku Hiva. The seafront at Papeete was bombed. In

1940, Tahiti and its dependencies rallied to General de Gaulle. Two years later, the Americans established an air base on Bora Bora, with a view to the reconquest of the Solomon Islands.

Little by little, Tahiti entered the modern world. The 1957 referendum gave the E.F.O. the status of Overseas Territory, granted a certain autonomy by the French constitution. The remake in 1961 of the film *Mutiny on the Bounty* with Marlon Brando (the original of 1934 starred Clark Gable), revived world interest in this little corner of paradise. Some 5,000 Tahitians were employed during filming, and for many it represented a return to their roots—but also a way of earning easy money.

In 1966, France chose the atoll of Mururoa, in the Tuamotu archipelago, to carry out its nuclear testing programme: 15,000 soldiers, technicians and bureaucrats converged on Tahiti, and Polynesia discovered the consumer society. Many families, attracted by the illusion of plenty, left the outlying islands for Papeete, where they were barely able to survive. Artificially inflated by the installation of the Pacific Experimental Centre, the standard of living rose to the highest in the Pacific after Hawaii. The extension of the airport in Faaa indirectly stimulated the tourist industry. In 1975, in response to pressure from the larger Pacific countries as well as locally, the French government abandoned atmospheric testing in favour of underground tests.

Towards Independence?

In 1984, a new statute granted increased autonomy to Polynesia, which henceforth had a Territorial Assembly and was represented in Paris by two deputies and a senator. When, in the autumn of 1995, President Chirac announced a series of nuclear tests (which had been frozen for ten years), the countries of the Pacific rim and ecological groups worldwide rose up in protest. Riots broke out in Tahiti. Initially enjoying little popular support, the independence movement led by Oscar Temauru, mayor of Faaa, became an important factor in Polynesian life, and the party won 11 of the 41 seats in the Assembly.

In 1996, internal autonomy was further increased. With the ending of nuclear tests, the future of the islands is uncertain. Opponents of independence point out that French Polynesia is not economically viable by itself: until now, France has guaranteed 90 per cent of the territory's budget.

An atoll in the Tuamotus: the life and death of an island.

On the Scene

Scattered over 4 million sq km (1.5 million sq miles) of ocean—a surface area equal to that of Europe—the islands are clustered into five archipelagos, which together scarcely total more than 4,300 sq km (1,600 sq miles) of dry land. The Society Islands, home to two-thirds of the population, comprise two groups: the five Windward Islands (Tahiti, Moorea, Maiao, Tetiaroa and Mehetia) and the Leeward Islands (Huahine, Raiatea, Tahaa, Bora Bora, Maupiti and other smaller islands). To the south, crossed by the Tropic of Capricorn, the Austral, or Tubuai, Islands are mountainous and do not all have a coral reef. The Tuamotu archipelago, which extends across nearly 1,500 km (900 miles) as far as the Gambiers, is the most numerous group of islands in French Polynesia and the only one to be formed entirely of atolls. The Marquesas, floating far off to the north of Tahiti, are a world apart.

TAHITI
Papeete, Around the Island

The jagged volcanic peaks of Tahiti and its sister isles are surrounded by the most beautiful lagoons in Polynesia. "Paradise on earth! It's paradise on earth!" was the stunned reaction of Bougainville's companions when they first set eyes on Tahiti one April morning in 1768.

Since its official discovery by European explorers more than two centuries ago, Tahiti has encapsulated the idea of a Polynesian Garden of Eden. The largest island of the archipelago, it covers an area of 1,042 sq km (402 sq miles). On the map, it looks a little like a frying pan, or a top-heavy figure of eight, of which the smaller loop, the Taiarapu Peninsula (also known as Tahiti Iti) lies southeast of the larger, almost circular Tahiti Nui, with the capital of French Polynesia, Papeete, on the north coast.

Papeete is today the fourth-largest town in the Pacific. Entering wholeheartedly into the modern era, it even has a rush hour morning and evening, and traffic jams they call the queue *(la file)*.

Tahiti's hinterland has retained all its charm. Beneath the majestic mountain peaks, the lush landscape is everything a tropical island should be, threaded by cascades and splashed by bright flowers: frangipani, hibiscus and *tiare*, the island's emblem, whose delicious scent fills the air.

Papeete

Tucked between the sea and the lower volcanic slopes of Mount Aorai, Papeete (pronounced *Papayaytay*) has fuelled the dreams of generations of seafarers. Its name means "basket of water", probably referring to the origins of the village as a source of fresh drinking water. Once a whaling station, it was chosen in 1844 as the place to set up the French administration. Today it's a thoroughly modern, commercial and cosmopolitan city with crowded thoroughfares. Boutiques, souvenir shops and restaurants have taken over the small streets in the centre. On the sea front, Boulevard Pomare, named after the last royal dynasty of Tahiti, is lined with blocks of low-rise apartment buildings. Troops parade along the boulevard for Bastille Day on July 14.

The old port, where schooners laden with copra once used to tie up, nowadays bustles with container ships, pleasure boats and ferries. Nevertheless, as the sun sets over the bay, you may still catch a glimpse of a canoe gliding silently over the water, against the dark silhouette of Moorea.

Sea Front

Opposite the Quai au Long-Cours, which closes the harbour where ships from all over the world and inter-island boats are moored, the sea front offers a pleasant promenade. South of the pier for ferries to Moorea is the Tourist Office, housed in Fare Manihini, a building in local style. Drop in for maps and brochures on all the islands.

Strolling westwards, you reach the post office and Bougainville Park. A bronze statue of the French explorer is flanked by two cannon, one recovered from the privateer of Count Felix von Luckner, sunk in 1916, the other from a French vessel that went down two years previously.

Continuing westwards, cross over Avenue Bruat, the most attractive street in town, and carry on to the Pearl Museum, in the shop called La Perle Noire. A video film and displays demonstrate how a pearl farm functions, and you will see finely crafted objects of mother-of-pearl as well as pearls of different shapes and colours.

Next door, Paofai Protestant church, built in 1873 and restored in 1980, is a magnificent colonial building: spiral staircases lead to the gallery from where you can take part in Sunday services. The men dress in their best black Sunday suits for the occasion, while the women sport wide-brimmed hats of woven pandanus and white dresses or capacious missionary frocks. Everyone joins in to sing *himenes*, moving polyphonic canticles in Tahitian, with intense fervour.

Town Centre

Behind the sea front, the town centre is a jumble of Chinese stores, souvenir shops and miscellaneous buildings totally lacking in charm. A few streets away from the fine town hall (Hôtel de Ville)—an "improved" copy of Queen Pomare IV's palace, inaugurated in 1990 for the town's centenary—is the covered market. This colourful array is at its most lively at dawn: by 8 a.m. things are already beginning to cool down. You can find almost anything amidst the general disarray and hurly-burly—fruit, vegetables, tropical flowers, live pigs and so on. The fish catch arrives in the late afternoon. The first floor is reserved for arts and crafts. Brightly painted lorries, called "trucks", set out from here to ply the roads of the island, delivering goods and serving as public transport.

Behind the Vaima shopping centre, the Catholic cathedral, adorned with modern stained-glass windows, was consecrated in 1875. A few streets further west stand the main public buildings—the Territorial Assembly, the residence of the High Commissioner and the Law Courts (Palais de Justice).

Around the Island

Round-the-island trips are an institution on Tahiti. At weekends, just about every islander sets out on scooter, car or truck to see what's happening elsewhere. The road circling the island covers 115 km (70 miles). If you want to explore Tahiti Iti (the smaller

1 THE BEST CHURCH SERVICE Attending the Sunday service at the **Paofai Church** in Papeete offers a unique opportunity to witness Polynesian religious fervour. Downstairs and on the balcony, men in black suits and women in white or coloured dresses sing hymns, canticles and psalms in the Tahitian language.

AROUND THE ISLAND

loop of the island's figure of eight, you can add an extra 20 km (12 miles) to reach Tautira on the north coast, and the same distance for Teahupoo on the south side.

The itinerary described below follows the route in an anti-clockwise direction and uses as a reference the "kilometric points" (PK) starting from Papeete.

West Coast

Tataa Point, 5 km (3 miles) west of Papeete, beyond Faaa airport and opposite Moorea, is the site of several luxury hotels. The most desirable residences in Tahiti line the western shore overlooking the lagoon, known as the "gold coast".

At PK11, the Lagoonarium, behind a bar and restaurant, comprises several glass-walled enclosures where you can observe the ballet of tropical fish and a couple of sharks. Feeding time is at noon each day.

A little further on, the white sands and coral outcrops at Toaroto (PK15) and Papehue (PK19) make these the most spectacular of the island's few beaches. All along the road, small stalls sell fruit and, at the end of the day, fish.

As you enter Punaauia, follow the arrow guiding you to the fascinating Museum of Tahiti and the Islands, standing in a park at the Pointe des Pêcheurs (Fisherman's Point). The museum is one of the most interesting in the South Pacific. The first room is devoted to the islands' natural habitat—their geological formation, flora and fauna. The history of Polynesia, its social and religious life and the daily round are covered in detail. The collection of ancient artefacts (canoes, magnificent *tikis*, finely wrought necklaces, weapons, etc.) provides an excellent overview of Polynesian culture. The last room covers the arrival of European explorers and missionaries.

At Paea, by the sea, the Polynesian-style Irihonu craft centre groups some of the best artisans on the island. Follow a small path through a discreet wooden gateway decorated with two *tikis* to reach the *marae* of Arahurahu, huddled in the shadow of the mountains. The site has been superbly restored. Originally it held no particular importance, but nowadays, ancient ceremonies are re-enacted during the July festivities. Some very fine *tikis* are on view.

At PK28.5, the Maraa Cave comprises two chambers, Vaipori and Matavaa. Vaipori, some 10 m (33 ft) high, encloses a small lake in a pretty setting of rocks and ferns.

The Musée du Coquillage at Papara (PK36), created by an avid

Around the Island

For singing hymns on Sunday, Papeete ladies wear missionary dresses and hats of woven pandanus.

collector, displays some 7,000 sea shells. Next door is a craft centre, the Maison de l'Artisanat.

The black sand Taharuu beach 3 km (2 miles) away is a favourite with Tahitian surfers. In the old days, this pastime was reserved for members of the aristocracy, the *ari'i*. The missionaries considered it to be futile and banned it. A short walk away, the Mahaiatea *marae* at Utumanomano Point was the largest in Tahiti. Captain Cook studied it closely, "struck with astonishment" at the deft workmanship of the neatly squared and polished coral slabs. He described it as a "pile of stonework raised pyramidically on an oblong base, like the roof of a house". The centre was filled with rounded pebbles, and a carved wooden bird stood on the ridge. Today, overgrown by vegetation, it looks just like a heap of stones. The tiny beach nearby, opening onto the lagoon, is one of the most pleasant on the island.

On Tahiti's widest plain, the 18-hole international golf course at Atimaono occupies the site of an old cotton plantation created during the American Civil War. At the time, the Confederate States were unable to supply the world market, causing cotton prices to rocket. A thousand Chinese were recruited to work the

Tahitian plantation. The boom ended after the war, when American production started up again. Around a hundred Chinese stayed on, their descendants representing 5 per cent of today's population.

The Gauguin Museum lies close to the sea, east of the village of Mataiea, where the painter lived during his first visit to Tahiti. It displays a large collection of archive documents and reproductions, but few original works of art—some wood engravings, two or three paintings and a fine lithograph of Prosper Mallarmé. The turbulent life of Gauguin is nevertheless recounted sensitively through a series of texts and photographs, from his earliest voyages when he signed up for the merchant navy, until his last days in the Marquesas. Three venerable *tikis* from the Austral Islands stand in the garden. The tallest is 2.72 m (almost 9 ft) high and weighs more than 2 tonnes. As everywhere in Polynesia, these statues of the ancestors are credited with supernatural powers. When the museum was inaugurated, they apparently refused to be transported, making themselves so heavy that no one could move them. The two largest, a "male" and a "female", are even rumoured to move closer together during the night.

On the same road, the Botanical Gardens at Motu Ovini were established by Harrison Willard Smith, an American physics professor who found peace only among flowers and trees. When he inherited a fortune after World War I, he bought this land and planted anything that took his fancy from all parts of the tropics. The eccentric amateur botanist is credited with introducing more than 200 new species of plants, both useful and decorative, to Tahiti. Here you can see huge ferns, giant bamboos, blazing canna plants, *mapes*—Tahitian chestnut trees with strangely contorted trunks—ponds brimming with lotus, and last but not least, two giant tortoises from the Galapagos.

At PK60, the road reaches Taravao, built on the isthmus separating Tahiti Nui from Tahiti Iti. From here, you have the choice of two roads into the peninsula.

Taiarapu Peninsula

Sparsely populated and relatively remote, Tahiti Iti offers a more traditional view of Polynesia. The western coast road reveals some lovely beaches (PK8), where fishermen's nets hang from the trees to dry. At the end of the road, you can join a boat trip to Tautira, which takes you round the southern tip of the island. You can also get there along a footpath that goes by way of the Te Pari cliffs (take a guide).

AROUND THE ISLAND

From Taravao, a second road leads to Tautira. A few beaches of black sand lie along the eastern coast, which is wilder than the northern shore. The village is one of the most traditional on Tahiti. The region is poorly served by road, so the preferred means of transport is still the canoe. A path, soon dwindling into a trail, leads down into the Vaitepiha Valley, following the course of the river of the same name. There are several archaeological sites along the way, against a spectacular backdrop formed by the craggy peaks of Mount Orofaamu. Beyond Tautira, another path, little used, takes you along the rocky coast. It is not long since this was home to the last *"hommes nature"*, Frenchmen for the most part, who had opted to return to nature and live like hermits along this deserted shore.

East Coast

Back on Tahiti Nui, the eastern shore, edged by high cliffs plunging straight into the sea, is much wilder than the west coast and has the most fantastic underwater scenery.

At Hitiaa, a favourite gathering point for surfers, a plaque commemorates the landing of Bougainville on August 6, 1768.

Once past Tiarei, a minor road leads by way of a luxuriant valley to the three great waterfalls of Te Faarumai. The first is easily accessible by means of a footpath climbing gently between *auti* plants. It is possible to swim here. Visiting the two other falls requires greater effort.

At Arahoho and its so-called Trou du Souffleur (Blowhole),

HEIVA

The festivities of Heiva last a whole month and celebrate internal autonomy, though officially they are supposed to commemorate Bastille Day (July 14). Until fairly recently, people still referred to it as Tiurai (derived from "July"). Heiva is the greatest annual festival of the territory, observed on all the islands but most fervently on Tahiti. There are several events arising from Polynesian tradition which take place in a fairground atmosphere: competitions for dancing, hymn-singing, hat-weaving, and bowls, football matches and such like, not to mention a hotly contested canoe race from Papeete to Moorea. But the most astonishing is perhaps the javelin contest: standing 30 m (100 ft) from the target, the competitors try to hit a coconut attached to a mast more than 10 m (30 ft) high. Heiva is also the time to get tattooed, as in the good old days.

AROUND THE ISLAND

the sea pounds into a rock crevice with such force that it covers the road from one side to the other in spray. Further on, at the eastern end of Matavai Bay is Venus Point, where on June 3, 1769, Captain Cook was able to observe the transit of Venus across the sun. A commemorative monument, a park and a lighthouse overlook one of Tahiti's most beautiful black sand beaches, very busy at weekends.

On the inland side of the road, a short distance before you get back to Papeete at PK6, you can't miss the colonial residence La Saintonge, built in 1892. Today it serves as Arue's elegant town hall. A short distance away, a signpost indicates the tomb of the last king of Tahiti. Hardly a heroic historic figure, Pomare V abdicated in exchange for a French pension and died of drink in 1891. The tomb, which held his mother's remains until he claimed it for his own, is distinguished by an unusual urn on the roof, which resembles nothing more than a huge red bottle of Benedictine liqueur.

The Interior

Rarely visited, even by the Polynesians, who believe it to be infested by *tupapaus* (the ghosts of their ancestors), the heart of the island is a confusion of razor-sharp summits and steep-sided valleys covered by a tangle of vegetation. Mount Orohena is the highest point in French Polynesia at 2,241 m (7,350 ft). On foot or by four-wheel-drive vehicle, you can visit numerous forgotten *maraes*, mysterious caves and superb waterfalls. Although some paths initially look suitable for a vehicle, they rapidly deteriorate. Since most of the land is privately owned, it is best to make tour arrangements through a specialized agency.

One of the most popular excursions is a drive to the top of Mount Marau, which overlooks Papeete from 1,493 m (4,898 ft). On the way, you'll see vegetables growing on the steep slopes; they belong to Chinese shopkeepers. Their ancestors began cultivation on the mountain at the end of the 19th century, since no land was available in the valleys. From the summit, there's a wonderful panorama of the capital, the reef and the island of Moorea.

The track crossing Tahiti from north to south, recently opened to four-wheel-drive vehicles, follows the Papenoo Valley to the heart of the island. It takes you near the Marama Nui dam, Maroto Valley (archaeological sites, and a small hotel) and Vaihiria lake, before descending to Mataiea on the south coast. Waterfalls cascade down the slopes all along the route.

TAHITI'S SISTER ISLES
Moorea, Huahine, Raiatea, Tahaa, Bora Bora, Maupiti, Tetiaroa

Moorea

For a thrilling introduction to the romance of the South Seas, you couldn't do better than rise at dawn as your ship glides into Cook's Bay. Thrusting green volcanic ridges ring a vast but placid bay; the peaks come in the most intriguing shapes—sand castle, pyramid, even a Gothic cathedral. As the sun rises, the shadows move and the colours change, revealing new fantasies. Windsurfers dart past yachts lolling at anchor in the crystal clear lagoon. Thatched huts extend to and beyond the water's edge. No one is in the slightest hurry on this magical isle, scarcely 20 km (12 miles) across the channel from the hubbub of Papeete.

On the map, Moorea resembles a butterfly—or the triangular fishtail that broke off from the original earth-fish when the archipelago was formed. Fishtail or not, Moorea means yellow lizard. Legends recount the exploits of elf-like lizard men, who would descend on the villages, kidnap women and steal anything they found useful. In fact, the whole of Moorea is steeped in legend. In the heart of the Opunohu Valley, dozens of ancient *maraes* are still waiting to be rediscovered.

Most of Moorea's 11,000 inhabitants live near the coast, fishing, farming, or working for the tourist dollar. Many commute by ferry to work in Tahiti. There are no real towns, only loosely-knit settlements, with a post office, a school, a church or two, and a Chinese-run general store, trailing off into relative wilderness until the next hamlet. Many wealthy Tahitians have moved over to Moorea to enjoy the peace and quiet. The laid-back lifestyle is centred on a handful of hotels and the luxurious straw huts of the Club Med, where the distant boom of the surf will lull you to sleep. Days are spent swimming, windsurfing or diving; as night falls you can sip a leisurely cocktail while waiting for dinner, often accompanied by Polynesian music and dance.

South Coast

A narrow road squeezed between the mountains and the shore runs all round the island, a distance of 60 km (37 miles). To help you get your bearings, large white mark-

The luxuriant mountains of Moorea form the backdrop to many films.

ers (PK) shaped like the island are planted every kilometre.

For those arriving by sea, the circuit begins at Vaiare. Planes land at Temae Airport, 4 km (2 1/2 miles) away, on the island's northeastern corner. The village of Temae has an obscure claim to fame. The American author Herman Melville turned up here in his early twenties after the most excruciating South Seas adventures—more than a year at sea aboard a whaling ship, desertion and life on the run, injury, mutiny and jail in Papeete. Once free in Moorea, Melville set off in search of local colour. He persuaded the village chief in Temae to defy the missionaries and permit the performance of an "indecent" dance known as Lory-Lory, the sexiest of all the Polynesian revels. It was all for a good cause, providing first-hand research material for the original South Seas novel, *Typee*.

There's a long sand-and-coral beach along the lagoon beyond the landing strip.

The island's administrative centre, Afareaitu, a quiet village 10 km (6 miles) to the south, may look like the customary collection of stores, office and a church, but it has some historical significance. The British missionaries who imposed Victorian morality in the South Seas settled here, founding a mission and school. Here they published the first book ever printed in Polynesia, a Bible. Here as on all the Society Islands, you will notice in front of each *fare* what appears to be a letter-box with a little roof. It is not for the mail, but for the baker to post his daily delivery of fresh bread. At the back of the village, a track leads to a beautiful waterfall.

The coast is thick with coconut palms. The aluminium rings you'll notice high on each trunk are not decorative or symbolic. They aim to block the path of high-climbing crabs and rats which would otherwise eat the coconuts.

Continuing round the island, there are miles of empty beaches

2 THE TWO MOST IMPRESSIVE MOUNTAINS There are many candidates for this title among Polynesian volcanoes. However, if we must name only two, then they have to be **Mount Mouaputa** on Moorea—the famous Shark's Tooth—and **Mount Otemanu** on Bora Bora, a sugar loaf rising straight out of the waters of the lagoon.

on the south and southwest coasts. The hamlet of Haapiti was the site of a Catholic mission, as you may guess from the unusually large church.

The coast is very sparsely populated from here to the northwest corner of Moorea, where a row of tourist resorts line the way. On a lagoon, Tiki Village was the brainchild of a Frenchman. Couples flock here from all over the world for a Polynesian-style wedding, tattooing ceremony included. But you don't have to get married to enjoy the dancing displays, demonstrations of crafts and copious banquets, *tamara'a*.

The hotels (Club Med among them) are set beneath the coconut palms along a magnificent beach of white sand. Excursions and diving expeditions are organized on the reef to see tropical fish and dolphins and to observe sharks feeding. Alternatively, you can go out in a glass-bottomed boat, take part in a fishing trip or a picnic on a *motu*.

North Coast

Papetoai, the "metropolis" of the north coast, is notable for the number of stately wooden colonial houses—called here "vanilla houses". They date from the 1930s, when fortunes were made in the production of vanilla. Papetoai was also a main base of the London Missionary Society; here King Pomare II was converted to Christianity in 1812, an event which hastened the demise of the traditional religion. The missionaries built an octagonal church on the site of an ancient *marae*; the present church was rebuilt a century ago. It is said to be the oldest European building still in use in the South Pacific.

Papetoai is the gateway to the enchanting Opunohu Bay, which thrusts deep into the centre of the island beneath the peaks of Mount Tohiea. Having no particular port town, it is secluded and well protected by the barrier reef dividing the aquamarine of the lagoon from the indigo sea beyond. Most of the recent version of *Mutiny on the Bounty*, starring Mel Gibson, was filmed here.

The island's other delightful north coast inlet is Cook's Bay. Just before you arrive there, turn off onto the little mountain road that takes you to the Moorea fruit juice factory, open for visits on weekdays. Tastings of fruit spirits and liqueurs, such as pineapple and guava, are included.

The arrival at Cook's Bay, with the loose conglomeration of Paopao at its head, is quite breathtaking. Great clouds drift apart to reveal a spectacular backdrop of mountains whittled by torrents into sharp jagged peaks. Cruise ships lie at anchor in the foreground. In the small Catholic church of St Joseph, a naïve wall-painting shows, as seen through Tahitian eyes, the angel exhorting Joseph and Mary to flee to Egypt. A small market is held very early every morning.

Opunohu Valley

By a track from Cook's Bay, or a tarred road from the head of Opunohu Bay winding inland into lush pastureland and tropical plantations, you reach Opunohu Valley, filling the collapsed crater of the ancient volcano. Before the arrival of the missionaries, the valley was a centre of population and religion. Archaeologists have found rich pickings here—some 500 structures in all. The biggest *marae* uncovered is that of Titiroa—in fact it's a complex of several. Construction, ordered by a warrior chief, dates back to the 18th century. The walls have been restored, but the volcanic stones are overgrown by a forest of *mape* trees whose rambling roots are lifting the paving. A bit higher, the *marae* of Afareaito, one of the best preserved of the valley, was erected after the victory of the Haapiti *ari'is* over those of Opunohu. The two platforms were used for archery competitions, reserved for nobles and warriors.

The valley road finally arrives at Roto Nui belvedere, from which you can sigh over the most spectacular panorama in French Polynesia. You look down the side of a volcanic crater where lava once flowed into the two captivating bays, divided by a rugged green peak, Mount Rotui. According to traditional belief, the souls of the dead assembled here before going to rest in the Windward Islands. Over to the east, you will easily recognize the silhouette of Mouaputa, Shark's Tooth mountain.

Coming back down to Paopao, make a stop at the Opuhi Plantation, pretty botanical gardens where there grows a profusion of *opuhi* (ginger flowers), vanilla orchids and other exotic plants.

Huahine

The great green, cloud-swathed hills of Huahine are rife with legend, history and mystery. The oldest traces of colonization of the Society Islands have been found here. Huahine is composed of two islands linked by a modern bridge over a channel between Maroe and Bourayne bays. Huahine Nui, the larger of the two, is the population centre. Legend has it that the god Hiro broke the island in two when crossing it with his canoe.

In Huahine all is beauty, luxury, calm and pleasure.

HUAHINE

Perhaps it was caused by the shock, or maybe it's just the capricious geology of volcanic islands, but Huahine's rugged coasts are deeply gouged by bays. Off the eastern shore, a few *motu* have been transformed into gardens, where melons and watermelons are cultivated. There are vanilla plantations on the main island.

Less than an hour by air from Papeete, the island has resisted tourism. For the lucky visitor, Huahine has some pleasant surprises—the turquoise lagoon, the lush hillsides blanketed in a dozen shades of green, the peace, but also the friendly welcome of its 5,400 inhabitants. After a few days here, you will understand why it is the Tahitians' favourite island.

Fare

The roads of Huahine follow its craggy contours, sometimes leaving the coast to wind inland. The town of Fare, on the northwest side of the island, is the model of a prosperous Polynesian village: trim bungalows surrounded by well-tended lawns and flower gardens. A good French-style highway is the main street through the business district, featuring the town hall, a modern post office, restaurants, jam-packed Chinese shops and some small hotels. Incidentally, some of the best surfing in French Polynesia may be found in Avamoa pass, off Fare. Most of the time, the town is as relaxing as an hour in a hammock. But when the freighters come in, delivering the necessities of life from Papeete, all the country folk seem to turn up for the excitement.

North of Fare, the Bali Haï Hotel includes a tiny museum consisting of two display cabinets. They hold artefacts dating from the 9th century, brought to light when the hotel was built: millstones, pestles, *patu* (whalebone war clubs), oystershell coconut graters, fish lures and hooks, and anchors for the giant Polynesian canoes. The excavation, led by Dr Yoshiko Sinoto, a respected archaeologist from Honolulu's Bishop Museum, is the biggest ever undertaken in the Society Islands. It uncovered a canoe building yard and threw light on the era of the great Polynesian transoceanic voyages.

Maeva

All of Huahine bears witness to the profundities of ancient Polynesian culture. The eight largest sanctuaries on the island (one for each of the traditional chiefdoms) are said to be founded by Princess Hutuhiva from Raiatea, who escaped from her native island in a drum. Before the Europeans arrived, the most important village of Huahine was Maeva, in the northeast corner of the island. All the district chiefs lived in close proximity here, and each had his own temple. It remains a key spiritual capital of Polynesia and several artists have chosen to live here.

Alongside the lagoon, the *fare pote'e*, a restored meeting house extending on stilts above the water, is now a fascinating museum with an astonishing collection of canoe paddles from every part of Polynesia. Close by is one of the many *maraes* recorded in the region.

Professor Sinoto discovered 35 *maraes* on Matairea Hill alone. The chiefs lived here in the 9th century, and each family had its own sanctuary. The site is reached after a two-hour climb up the jungle-clad slopes, through vanilla and banana plantations.

Fauna Nui lagoon is linked to the ocean by a shallow gully where you will notice strange V-shaped stones. They are ancient fish traps, in use as they have been for centuries. Fish carried by the tide are funnelled into the specially constructed rocks, tripping a wooden trapdoor. The catch is not for sale; it is for the use of Maeva residents only.

Out on Papiti motu, opposite the village, Manunu *marae* was a communal sanctuary for Huahine Nui. Its two-level platform (*ahu*) was used for the worship of Tane, god of war and of fish, before he was supplanted in the 17th century by Oro, a god from Raiatea. Sofitel Heiva hotel is on the same *motu*, which has a long beach of coral and white sand, swept by breakers.

From the track linking Maeva to Huahine Iti bridge, a lookout provides a stunning view over Maroe Bay.

Huahine Iti

A road of crushed coral circles the island, past palm-fringed lagoons. At Parea, the southernmost point of Huahine Iti, the two-level Anini *marae* was dedicated to Hiro (god of thieves) and to Oro. Human sacrifices were carried out here. Parea's pretty beaches serve several hotels. On the west coast, look out for the fabulous Hana Iti Hotel—some of its bungalows, inspired by the Polynesian *fare*, are built in the trees above Haapu Bay.

Raiatea

Two islands in the same lagoon, Tahaa and Raiatea are usually mentioned in the same breath, like beauty and charm. The larger is Raiatea, which means "serene skies". Mountainous in the south, it lies 40 km (25 miles) west of Huahine and is the biggest and most densely populated of the Leeward Islands, with 10,000 in-

RAIATEA

The village of Uturoa and the northeast point of Raiatea are visible from Mount Tapioi.

habitants for 170 sq km (66 sq miles). Compensating for the narrowness of its coastal plains, wide verdant valleys cut into the hillsides. At the open passes in the reef, the waves have scoured out deep bays, such as Faaroa.

Raiatea is Polynesia's sacred isle and its cultural, political and religious capital. The ancients called it Havai'i. Priests from all over Polynesia used to meet here, for the island's *maraes* were held to be the most powerful of all. The chiefs of the Tamatoa dynasty, believed to be descendants of the gods, possessed almighty power. For centuries they presided over the destiny of the Society Islands. Raiatea was the starting point for the incredible canoe migrations to Easter Island and New Zealand. In the late 19th century, a Raiatea chief, Teraupo, made a name for himself in Paris by holding out against French rule. Long after the other islands had accepted the French protectorate, the rebellious local forces defied all efforts at pacification. French troops landed in 1897 to establish control; it took them six weeks to subdue Teraupo.

Uturoa

The commercial and administrative capital of the Leeward Islands, Uturoa is Polynesia's second-largest town, with 3,000 inhabitants. The underpinnings of modern urban life are well established; a hospital and power station, post office and pharmacy, police station and courthouse, stores, cafés and billiards hall. There's a lively mercantile atmosphere in the rows of Chinese-run stores, each filled with an amazing array of goods.

The old-fashioned covered market wakes up early in the morning, when fishermen and farmers come in to sell their produce. It is all over by 7.30 a.m.

Behind the town, four-wheel-drive vehicles can breeze to the top of Mount Tapioi: the view takes in neighbouring Tahaa and the perpetual wonders of the blue-green lagoon and ultramarine South Pacific.

Near the airport, the small Na Te Ara Museum displays a collection of shells, and tropical fish in glass tanks. Past the airport, Apooiti's marina has the largest flotilla of yachts for hire in all the Society Islands. The ancient rite of fire-walking was performed here. Volcanic stones would be heated for several hours before the ceremony began—a demonstration of mind over matter.

Around the Island

A partially surfaced road some 100 kilometres (60 miles) long circles the island. Most of the hotels are clustered along the luxuriant eastern shore. Here and there you'll notice copra drying-sheds with corrugated iron roofs.

Shortly after Avera, Faaroa Bay cuts deep inland. A popular excursion goes from there up the Apoomau, the only navigable river in French Polynesia, in a powerboat or motorized outrigger canoe. The Apoomau narrows into the steamy essence of a primeval tropical waterway, with fishermen's stilt cottages isolated along the banks. The trip usually includes a picnic or a stop for bathing on one of the *motus* in the lagoon between the river mouth and the reef. You can circumnavigate the *motu* in a leisurely ten-minute hike, or walk across it, beneath the shade of the coconut palms, in half the time. The swimming and snorkelling are worth the detour.

Beyond the village of Opoa, where vanilla is still cultivated, stand the remains of the monumental Taputapuatea *marae*. Its great size alone reveals the importance of this ancient site. Here, at the edge of the lagoon, facing the Te Ava Moa pass, the great chiefs and lesser nobles came to worship Oro, the god of war. The aristocracy of Taputapuatea had the power of life or death over all newborn children. One of the enclosures was reserved for the priests, the other

RAIATEA • TAHAA

for the aristocracy, where you can still see the stone backrests of the highest-ranking celebrants. Joseph Banks, the naturalist who sailed on the *Endeavour* with Captain Cook, described the *marae* as being different from those on Tahiti, its walls, some 8 ft high, being built of enormous blocks of coral. In a large house nearby, they saw a small canoe, to which eight human lower jawbones were attached. Tupia (the Maohi guide of the expedition) explained that it was traditional to display the jawbones of warriors killed in combat.

TIARE

A unique flower, the *tiare apetahi*, grows on Raiatea at an altitude of 800 m (2,600 ft) on the upper slopes of the Temehani volcano—said to be the birthplace of the god Oro. The unusual flower looks as though it has been cut in two as it has only a half-corolla, all five petals clustered together on one side. To see them growing, you have to climb the volcano beyond the waterfalls and stands of bamboo, as botanists have never succeeded in making it take root elsewhere. The flowers open in the early morning with a characteristic crackle. If you hear it, you will be blessed with perpetual good fortune.

To the south, a pretty little beach slopes gently into the turquoise waters.

Beyond the *marae*, the road degenerates into a track, running parallel to the shore and providing an exceptional view over the lagoon and pass from Puutarape Point.

The island's southern coast is planted with coconut groves, gradually giving way to brooding mountains and thickening vegetation. From the head of Faatemu Bay, sheltered by black cliffs, a road crosses the island to Faaroa Bay. From the southwest coast you can see a string of *motu*, close to shore. At Tevaitoa, on the way back to Uturoa, you pass the Tainuu *marae*, whose great stones resemble menhirs.

Tahaa

Known as the Vanilla Isle, Tahaa is not as unspoiled as a *motu*, but no one has yet complained that it's overexploited. Most visitors are day-trippers from Raiatea. There's no landing strip: ferries and schooners link the sister islands, only 5 km (3 miles) apart, a journey of some 20 minutes. The arrival of bigger freighters from as far afield as Bora Bora or Tahiti always creates a stir.

Tahaa has no modern buildings or large hotels, only a few quiet little fishing villages. The coastline is indented, as if the ocean has taken great bites from the shores. The surrounding lagoon is one of the most beautiful in all Polynesia.

Tahaa is not as green and fertile as Raiatea, for the smaller island is less mountainous, attracting fewer rainclouds. But the air is filled with fragrance. *Vanilla tahitensis*, said to be the best vanilla in the world, is cultivated here. The first plants were introduced in 1848, and intensive cultivation began in the 1890s. On a visit to a plantation, you will learn how extremely difficult it is to produce the precious pods from the plant, which only give off their heady perfume after being processed and dried. Tahaa produces 70 per cent of Polynesian vanilla.

A road snakes along the coast, completing the circuit of the island in 67 km (42 miles). From the Taira Pass, don't miss the view over two bays, Hurepiti in the west and Haamene in the east. The population, estimated at 4,000 inhabitants, less than half that of Raiatea, is scattered along the coast, essentially at Patio in the north, the island capital.

Every October, the islanders still organize "stone fishing"—the fishermen in canoes beat the water with stones, driving the fish towards the shore where they are caught in nets or palm-frond traps. The event is the occasion for a big feast, when elaborate dishes are cooked in an underground oven.

Excursions, including fish barbecues on the beach, take you to visit one of the idyllic *motus* off the north of the island or one of the new pearl farms in Haamene Bay.

Bora Bora

When you see a photo summing up Polynesia, the scene is usually Bora Bora; islands don't come any lovelier. Ocean waves brush the barrier reef, the lagoon beyond shimmers in hues from deepest amethyst to palest turquoise, lapping the perfect silver crescent of beach. A strangely emotive volcanic peak, sculpted and scored by the wind and rains over 7 million years, scrapes the wispy clouds.

Situated 240 km (150 miles) from Tahiti, the "Pearl of the Pacific", as Captain Cook called it, is tiny: a mere 9 km (5 1/2 miles) from one end to the other, and 4 km (2 1/2 miles) wide. The population hovers around 5,800, hardly enough to make a crowd. They live in three villages: Vaitape, the capital, Anau and Faanui. Bora Bora, Cook's spelling, is difficult for the Polynesians to pronounce, since there is no letter B in their language; Pora Pora is more like it. Incidentally, they pronounced Cook "Toote".

BORA BORA

For many years, bitter struggles opposed the tribes of the three main districts of the island, known at that time as Vava'u or Mai Te Pora. When King Puni finally unified the island, shortly before the arrival of Cook, a dispute began with Raiatea for political and religious supremacy in the Leeward Islands. On Raiatea, they said, the inhabitants were fearsome, the women ugly and, worst of all, they did not own a single pig between them!

Before the Europeans arrived, there were 42 *maraes* on the island, several of which have been restored. They were abandoned when missionaries arrived; by 1822 there was a church at Vaitape. To this day Bora Bora has a higher percentage of Protestants than the other islands.

The greatest upheaval in Bora Bora's history was its "discovery" by the US Navy in World War II. An airstrip was built, the first in French Polynesia, and a logistical base, finally destined to play no great part in the war. The 5,000 GIs, stationed on the island—including the author James Michener—had no complaints: they were surrounded by friendly people in a lovely refuge, and the battles stayed thousands of miles away. Virtually overnight, electricity and dollars came on the scene, not to mention a few fair-haired children. In the face of this new prosperity, the islanders soon abandoned copra and vanilla cultivation.

Thirty years later, the Americans returned. This time it was Dino de Laurentis, who came to film *Hurricane*. Since then, the island has embraced its new destiny, and hotels, built in the traditional *fare* style, have mushroomed all round the lagoon. The island economy has been turned upside down as a result. Some may miss its old-fashioned charm, but Bora Bora remains one of the Pacific's leading tourist destinations.

Vaitape

The island's main town and administrative centre is reached by boat from the airport, which is on a *motu* to the north of the lagoon (free shuttle service). It lies at the foot of Mount Pahia, opposite Te Ava Nui pass and the isle of Toopua (said to be the petrified canoe of Hiro, the god of Bora Bora).

Vaitape has a couple of shops, a red-spired Protestant church and nearby, a tiny blue Catholic church. On Sunday mornings, the bells ring out seemingly endlessly, summoning the faithful.

The imposing silhouette of Mount Otemanu dominates the eastern coast.

BORA BORA

Near the quayside, right next to the Craft Centre *(Bora Bora i te fanu tahi)* is the discreet tomb of Alain Gerbault (1893–1941), a French adventurer famed for sailing single-handedly around the world aboard the *Firecrest* between 1923 and 1929. He died in Timor during World War II, and his body was brought back to Bora Bora six years later.

During the *Heiva* festival in July, palm huts spring up all over the village, and a fairground atmosphere prevails, with canoe races and dancing competitions.

For a superb panorama of the lagoon, the ring of *motu* and the neighbouring islands of Tupai, Maupiti and Tahaa, climb Mount Pahia—a stiff 3-hour hike.

Around the Island

Hire a bicycle and set off to tour the island. World War II buffs can climb a hill north of Vaitape to inspect two rusting coastal artillery guns which defended the strategic Te Ava Nui pass, the way into the lagoon. It took 400 men almost five months to haul them up with ropes.

Beyond Pahua Point, the Yacht Club has become a mecca for yachtsmen sailing the Pacific. Leaving the pier where the ferries are docked, the road curves inward to follow Faanui Bay, site of the Taianapa *marae*, restored in 1963. The area surrounding Faanui village was the centre of American military operations in the 1940s. North of the bay, by the roadside, the Fare Opu *marae* is notable for its easily decipherable stone carvings portraying turtles, which were used as special sacrifices in pagan rites. Only kings and priests had the right to eat their flesh. Before the Europeans arrived, the *marae* was considerably bigger, but in the 1820s, missionaries used much of its stone to build a quay at Vaitape.

At PK11, beyond the northern tip of the island, the small Marine Museum contains two dozen models of famous ships, some associated with Polynesian history such as the *Bounty* and the *Endeavour*.

On the wilder east coast, the village of Anau is attractively set in a décor of coconut palms and banana trees, against the singular backdrop of Mount Otemanu, the highest point on Bora Bora.

Matira Point

South of Vaitape, the road follows the curve of Povaie Bay. Some odd bits of wartime memorabilia are gathered in what's known as Tatu's Museum: a local eccentric has put on display a rusted 8-inch coastal cannon and two anchors, all salvaged from the lagoon at his expense, plus the remains of military vehicles.

Most of Bora Bora's luxury hotels are located around Raititi, Matira and Paopao points, on a spit of land pointing south towards the reef. Matira Beach, along the small road signposted Moana Beach Hotel, is unquestionably one of the loveliest in the world, its glistening white sand gently sloping into a perfectly transparent lagoon. It's ideal for children, floaters, snorkellers or swimmers of any stripe. Fringing the shore are elegant palms, hibiscus and frangipani trees. Nearby, you can jet ski, water ski, try parascending or hire a yacht or a motor boat.

Immediately behind the Matira hotel, follow the steepish path to discover two cannon set up by the Americans in 1942–43. You can also admire a view of both sides of Matira Point.

The Lagoon

Organized excursions include tours on the lagoon all round the island, usually accompanied by a picnic on a *motu* and the possibility of watching sharks feeding. Other options are deep-sea fishing or a trip in a glass-bottomed boat to enjoy the extraordinary colours of the sea bed. The coral gardens abound with giant clams, angelfish, parrotfish, manta rays, toadfish and so on.

You could also hire an outrigger canoe and row to a deserted *motu*, gliding silently across the lagoon. One of easiest for landing is Taurere, opposite Matira Point, hemmed by a frill of white sands. In the shelter of Tupititi Point, strong swimmers can venture into a fascinating labyrinth of multi-coloured coral. You can also explore Tofari *motu*, which protects the eastern side of Bora Bora from the Pacific breakers. Tupe *motu*, an extension of Tofari, has been turned into a Lagoonarium, where sharks, turtles and rays swim around in pens.

If you sail past Piti Aau *motu*, you may be intrigued by the dome-shaped *fares*. They were erected by a sect that settled here some years ago, expecting the arrival of extraterrestrials.

Opposite Vaitape, the little Tapu *motu* was chosen by the German film director F.W. Murnau in 1928 as the setting for his documentary film *Tabu*, the very first to bring Polynesia to the silver screen. The island elders opposed the filming as the location had previously been a sacred site reserved for the royal family. Murnau made the film anyway. Perhaps they put a curse on him. Back in New York, he was killed in a car accident just before the opening night.

The French polar explorer Paul-Emile Victor lived in a house on Tane *motu*, close to the airport.

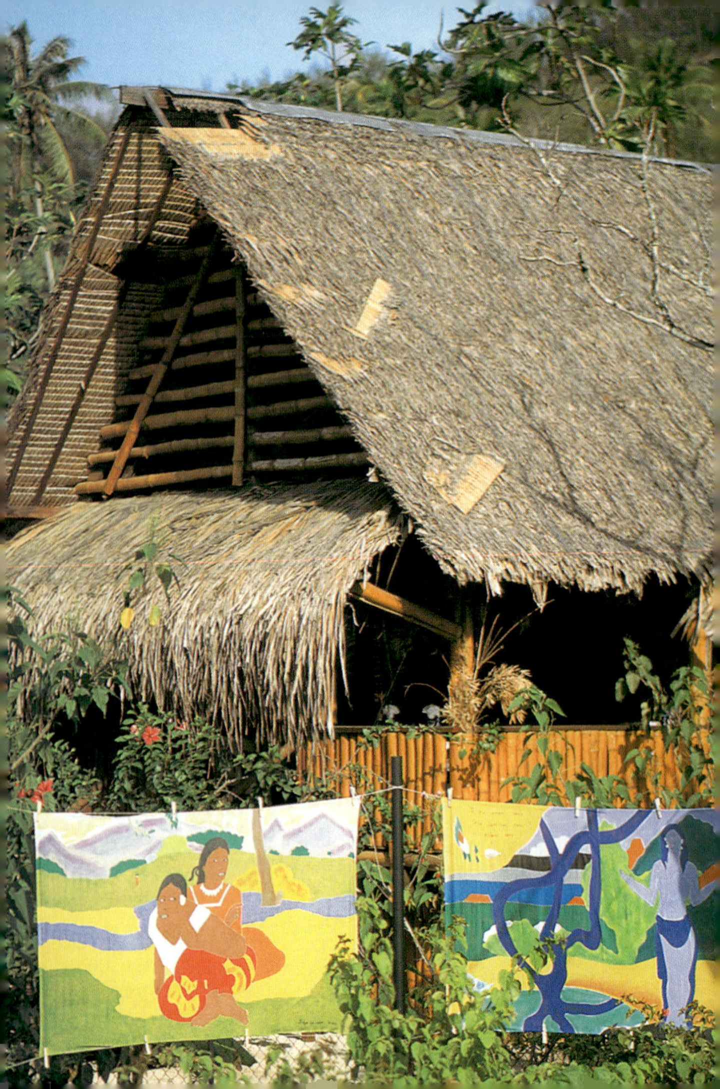

Maupiti

Set in an emerald lagoon, the tiny island of Maupiti, some 40 km (25 miles) west of Bora Bora, is an uncommonly spectacular juxtaposition of low-slung *motus* surrounding a high-rise volcanic island with majestic cliffs. The highest point is Mount Teurafaatiu, at 372 m (1220 ft). With fewer than 1000 inhabitants, and no hotels, Maupiti is hardly ready for tourism. But its splendid scenery and sparkling white beaches are too perfect to remain hidden much longer.

Most of the people live in the village of Vaiea. They live from fishing and cultivating copra, while taro, manioc and watermelons are grown on the *motus*. The island is reputed for the pass in the reef, one of the most dangerous in all Polynesia, and for its numerous *tupapaus*, the spirits of the dead. The people have even decreed a festival day in their honour.

Since the landing strip was opened in 1975, Maupiti has gradually opened up to the outside world. But accommodation is available only in private homes, and activities are limited to exploration of the five *motus*, fishing expeditions in the jade-green lagoon, snorkelling in the coral gardens, and a walk around the island, which you can complete in three hours if you take your time. On the way, everyone you meet will say hello. Of the island's 60 *maraes*, note in particular Vaiahu, beside the lagoon. There are rock carvings of turtles in the Haranae Valley.

Tetiaroa

Lying 42 km (26 miles) north of Papeete, barely 20 minutes of flying time, this island is actually an atoll made up of 13 *motu* surrounding a delightful lagoon. Before the actor Marlon Brando bought Tetiaroa in 1966 on a 99-year lease, it was known for its historic role as the holiday home, and occasional political retreat, for the kings of Tahiti. The last king, Pomare V, gave the island to a Welshman, Dr Williams, in lieu of medical fees.

Marlon Brando fell in love with the island and decided to buy it after filming *Mutiny on the Bounty*. Under the spell of Polynesia, he even married his Tahitian partner Tarita.

Comfortable bungalows are available for stays on the island, and you can spend your time enjoying the diving. A popular excursion is to Tahuna Iti, the "island of birds", where frigate birds, gannets and crested terns nest in the sand.

Gauguin's paintings inspire Polynesian pareos.

TUAMOTU AND GAMBIER ISLANDS
Rangiroa, Manihi, Tikehau, Gambier Islands

Until the 1960s, when the French began testing atomic bombs at Mururoa atoll, the sprawling Tuamotu archipelago hardly rippled the consciousness of the rest of the world. For centuries before that, ironically, it had been known as the Dangerous Archipelago because of its badly charted reefs and unpredictable sea currents.

Thankfully, the nuclear tests have been abandoned, and the islanders are ready to offer the warmest of welcomes to any visitor fascinated by the beauty of the ocean. Two luxury hotels in the form of bungalows and a number of small family guesthouses provide hospitality.

The archipelago extends for more than 1,000 km (600 miles), making it the largest island group in the world. Its total land area comes to about 855 sq km (330 sq miles). All but one of the dozens of isles comprising the Tuamotu ("ocean islands") are coral atolls, barely peeking above the waterline, their shores lapped by crystal-clear wavelets.

Below, the submarine sights are a festival of colour. Most divers also know that, beneath the silence and apparent calm, the Tuamotu offer the distinct possibility of a thrilling encounter with a shark. There is a long tradition here of diving without oxygen.

The Paumotu—as the inhabitants are known—live from the ocean, which is their only asset. Bonito and caranx, and even the occasional small shark, are driven into pens by the tides. Copra has been more or less abandoned in favour of the more lucrative culture of black pearls. Agriculture is virtually non-existent, as soil is a rare commodity on a coral island—to the point where some Paumotu have it shipped over from Tahiti in order to grow their vegetables.

Rangiroa

The ancient Polynesians called it Rairoa, or "long sky". As you approach the atoll, the eternal colour scheme appears, as on a fanciful flag of the South Pacific: blue, white and green, for the sea, the strip of sand, and the bristly green line of coconut palms. Once past the tricky channel through the reef, the immensity of Rangiroa becomes apparent. The lagoon is so big you can't see the other side, so big that the island of Tahiti itself could fit inside. The atoll lies about as low in the water as a rowboat.

Rangiroa is the paragon of desert isles, the type of place to

The blue lagoon of Rangiroa: paradise regained?

visit if you have all the time in the world. There are buildings enough to house a population of 1900, but no structure is taller than a palm tree.

The atoll offers a wide variety of water-based sports and activities. It is a paradise for divers, anglers and anyone who dreams of leaving a footprint for Robinson Crusoe to discover.

Villages

There are two villages, their houses painted in warm colours. At the western end of the biggest *motu,* Tiputa is the administrative centre. But it is on the other side of the channel, on Avatoru *motu,* 8 km (5 miles) long, where most of the population is clustered, along with the hotels, guesthouses, airport, school and so on. You can easily complete the tour of the isle in half an hour by bicycle, or even quicker by scooter.

Alongside the only road, bordered by frangipani, *tiare* and hibiscus, fishermen and their wives sell the day's catch as evening falls: surgeonfish, parrotfish or other exotic species. On Sundays, almost everybody goes to church.

The Gauguin pearl farm at Avatoru is open for visits every morning from Monday to Saturday.

The Lagoon

Two channels cut through the reef, the steeper being Tiputa, 400 m (1,300 ft) wide. Here, at a depth of 20 m (65 ft), the close encounter with sharks has become a classic feature of diving at Rangiroa. The instructor attracts the sharks with a few dainty morsels, unleashing a collective frenzy. A few giant manta rays join in the fray, along with shoals of cofferfish, parrotfish and mullet in multi-coloured, glittering clouds.

The groupers of Hiria Channel are famous for their great size, the largest specimens weighing over 100 kg (220 lb). The smallest fish, the *kito*, invade the lagoon in

BLACK PEARLS

Pearl farming is the third-largest industry in Polynesia. It employs 5,000 workers on 300 farms, which handle more than a million pearls each year. The most highly prized, the Tuamotu black pearl, is produced by the giant black-lipped *Pinctada margaritifera cumingi*, four times bigger than the Japanese *akoya* oyster, from which most white pearls are obtained.

At one time, Paumotu divers used to fish for pearls by diving without breathing apparatus to depths as great as 50 m (160 ft) in order to retrieve a few oysters. Brought to the surface, only one in 10,000 produced a pearl. During the 1970s, the culture of pearl oysters was developed. The technique was invented by the Japanese in the immediate post-war years. The oysters are hatched in the lagoon; when they are three years old, each one is grafted by hand. A round, polished nucleus a few millimetres in diameter, taken from Mississippi clams, is introduced by incision into the gonad of the oyster. On this nucleus is placed a piece of tissue taken from another oyster, which subsequently forms the sac in which the mother-of-pearl is produced. If all goes well, a pearl will have formed within two or three years. However, out of a hundred oysters grafted, only half survive, 40 produce a pearl, of which 20 are saleable and only five considered to be flawless. The currents, the water temperature, its salinity and mineral content all play an important part in creating the pearl and determining its lustre and colour, which can vary from pale silver to dark black, with overtones in all the colours of the rainbow: blues and greens, pinks and purples, orange, gold and shimmering bronze ("fly's wing").

tight shoals during the month of June before dispersing at the next full moon. You can survey the whole scene from a glass-bottomed boat.

When you have seen enough of the sea bed, or you prefer your air warm and fresh rather than bottled, take a trip to one of the atoll's countless *motu*. In a few minutes or in a few hours (the lagoon is so huge that the choice is infinite), the boat will carry you away to a beach of dazzling white sand. A few yards from the shore the water is so clear that you can easily distinguish the silhouettes of young sharks. If the Paumotu are to be believed, there is no reason to worry—they all played with sharks as children and lived to tell the tale.

A favourite destination is the Taeo'o *motu* or Blue Lagoon, a 45-minute trip. In this fabulous group of desert isles, set out in a circle, the classic images of Polynesia materialize: turquoise water at 30°C (86°F), clusters of coconut palms, white fairy terns gliding above and brown gannets nesting on the ground. You can walk on the rocks from one *motu* to the next. When you leave, the remains of your picnic will attract dozens of greedy black-tipped reef sharks.

Two other excursions are available, one to the pink sands of Vahituri at the eastern end of the lagoon (the trip takes 90 minutes to 2 hours), the other to the nearer Ile aux Récifs (Reef Island), and its remarkable fossilised coral formations.

Manihi

In 1722, the Dutch Admiral Jacob Roggeveen, who first discovered Easter Island, named it Aurora. The inner lagoon of 100 sq km (40 sq miles) is an almost perfect ellipse 60 km (37 miles) in circumference, rivalling Rangiroa's lagoon for beauty. The water temperature never dips below 28°C (82°F). This is probably one of the secrets of success of the farms that produce Polynesia's "black gold"—cultured pearls. The very first was set up here in the 1970s. The oysters grow in cages to protect them from predators, while cohorts of rainbow-coloured fish dart in and out of the coral. Robert Wan, the "pope" of the black pearl, has more than a million oysters on this atoll alone.

The growth in pearl farming has brought about a population explosion. The number of inhabitants practically tripled in a few years, from 400 to 1150. Supplies arrive by plane from Tahiti; the people come to the airport to collect their goods and take them home by boat, some to the nearby village of Turipoa, others to a private *motu*.

Pearl Beach resort, where bungalows have been built partly over the lagoon, is evidence that Manihi has been discovered by the tourist industry. Divers in particular appreciate the exceptional underwater scenery. On several *motu* at the far end of the atoll, you'll find wonderful sandy beaches perfect for picnics or fishing.

Manihi's smaller neighbour is Ahe. In the absence of an airstrip or a tourist hotel, it's an island stripped to the essentials, where the locals eke out a living by fishing and harvesting coconuts.

Tikehau

Tikehau exemplifies the unspoilt nature of the Tuamotu Islands. Some claim it to be the most beautiful atoll in Polynesia. The lagoon forms almost a perfect circle, and will delight divers and anglers—when Jacques Cousteau studied it in 1987 he found it had more fish than any other lagoon in the Tuamotu. Excursions are available to the coral islets for an unforgettable picnic or to visit the fish pens, which are still the principal source of revenue for the island's 400 inhabitants.

Gambier Islands

The most far-flung archipelago of French Polynesia, the Gambier group is closer to Pitcairn, the island adopted by the *Bounty* mutineers, than to Tahiti, more than 1,800 km (1,000 miles) away. It comprises eight islands and some 20 islets with a total surface area of just 36 sq km (14 sq miles). The population is confined to Mangareva ("the floating mountain"), a verdant isle dominated by Mount Duff, 441 m (1,447 ft) high. When the Polynesian islands were ruled by kings, the successor to the throne of Man-

3 THE THREE BLUEST LAGOONS Images of **Bora Bora**'s lagoon are familiar all over the world, and it's true that for colour, no other can surpass it. Except, perhaps, the **Blue Lagoon** of Rangiroa in the Tuamotu, which is irresistibly gorgeous: warm waters of a marvellous limpidity and dazzling turquoise hues, scarcely more than a couple of fathoms deep; white sands; isles crowned with coconut palms. Within the same group of atolls, the **Manihi** lagoon, famous for its pearl oysters, offers divers the opportunity to explore a submarine world of staggering beauty.

gareva had to live as a recluse in the mountains until his time came to reign.

In the 19th century, the island came under the control of Father Laval, a Catholic missionary who ruled with a rod of iron. It was he who built the immense coral cathedral, the largest in Polynesia, which still stands on Rikitea.

The island slumbers languidly most of the time, awakened only once a month when the supply ship from Papeete comes into port—and therein lies its charm.

Most of the 1,000 inhabitants cultivate coffee, oranges or watermelons, or work for the pearl farm—local conditions are ideal for the production of black pearls with a green opalescence. You can look around the farm, in addition to a workshop for engraving on mother-of-pearl run by the brethren of the Sacred Heart.

If you want to visit Mangareva, you need to apply for permission from the Subdivision of the Tuamotu and Gambier Islands, in Papeete.

MURUROA

In 1964, the Polynesian Territorial Assembly granted the French government full rights over two atolls situated 1,200 km (745 miles) east of Tahiti—Mururoa and Fangataufa. With Algerian independence, France had been obliged to reduce its activities in the Sahara and was looking to the Pacific to continue its testing of nuclear weapons. Two years later, the first atmospheric tests began. Thermonuclear charges were tested on Fangataufa in 1968. In 1975, international pressure forced the government to turn to underground testing: narrow vertical holes were laboriously bored deep into the coral islands to receive the nuclear charges. Tests were frozen during the 1980s and restarted in 1995 by order of President Chirac—for the last time, it has been maintained—provoking public condemnation around the world. The consequences of these 181 controversial explosions are difficult to evaluate. Whereas the French Atomic Energy Commission is reassuring, antinuclear associations are concerned about the geological security of the atoll. The atoll's porous basalt foundations were weakened by the blasts and could in the long term release radioactive nuclei into the waters of the Pacific. The military authorities say this process could take 500 to 1,500 years. It is worth bearing in mind, however, that plutonium, 20 kg (44 lb) of which lie at the bottom of the lagoon, has a half-life of 24,000 years.

AUSTRAL ISLANDS
Rimatara, Rurutu, Tubuai, Raivavae, Rapa

The five Austral Islands straddle the Tropic of Capricorn in a chain stretching across 1,300 km (800 miles) of ocean. They form the most southerly and least well-known archipelago of French Polynesia, lying between 500 and 1,000 km (300 and 600 miles) south of Tahiti. The climate is more temperate here, and the enterprising inhabitants produce great quantities of vegetables, coffee and tropical fruit which supply the rest of the territory. They are also renowned for their basket-making.

From west to east, Rimatara, Rurutu, Tubuai, Raivavae and Rapa are all inhabited. Their remoteness has ensured the survival of many ancient Polynesian customs. For example, during festivals on Rurutu, the men still compete in stone-lifting contests, where the biggest stones weigh up to 150 kg (330 lb).

Rimatara
Rimatara is the most westerly of the Austral Islands and has no port, no hotels, no guesthouses—and no alcohol. It can be reached only by boat, and even then the whaler has to count on the help of a large breaker to lift it over the reef. It's hardly surprising, then, that Rimatara is rarely visited. With its 8 sq km (3 sq miles) it is the smallest island of the archipelago.

Rurutu
Unprotected by a coral reef, Rurutu is wild and mountainous, its highest peak, Mount Taatioe, culminating at 389 m (1,276 ft). The island emerged from the sea bed 12 million years ago and was enlarged a million years ago after a residual eruption. Consequent erosion has sculpted the landscape and formed a network of caves. You can visit the Anaaeo Grotto, known for its stalagmites. The inhabitants of Rurutu are renowned for the quality of their wood carving. The ideal way of exploring the island's craggy terrain is on horseback.

Tubuai
Administrative centre of the archipelago, this is the largest of the Austral Islands and probably the most beautiful. Surrounded by a turquoise lagoon and a barrier reef dotted with coral islands, it has magnificent beaches of white sand. Oranges, peaches and coffee are cultivated here. This was the first port of call of the *Bounty* mutineers before they finally decided to settle on Pitcairn Island. The ruins of Fort George,

When the sun sinks below the horizon, the shooting stars appear.

which they built in 1789, can still be seen near the port. A road 24 km (15 miles) long girdles the island.

Raivavae

The island where time stands still, Raivavae barely covers 16 sq km (6 sq miles). Mountainous and blanketed in tree ferns, it is encircled by a coronet of a dozen *motus* where seabirds nest. The huge stone *tikis* in the Gauguin Museum on Tahiti came from Raivavae; their style, according to archaeologists, represents an intermediary stage between those of the Marquesas and the Easter Island statues.

Rapa

Last stop before the Antarctic, Rapa is the remotest of all. Its southerly latitude means the temperature may drop to 5°C (40°F) in July and August. Its Maohi name, Rapa Iti, suggests a link with Rapa Nui—Easter Island. The two villages (500 inhabitants) are linked by a 10-km (6-mile) road. You can climb up to the ruins of terraced stone fortresses, *pa,* built on the mountain summits, and thought to be the vestiges of long-forgotten tribal wars. Boats bring supplies only once every month or two. The choir is famous: their music is said to be the oldest in the world.

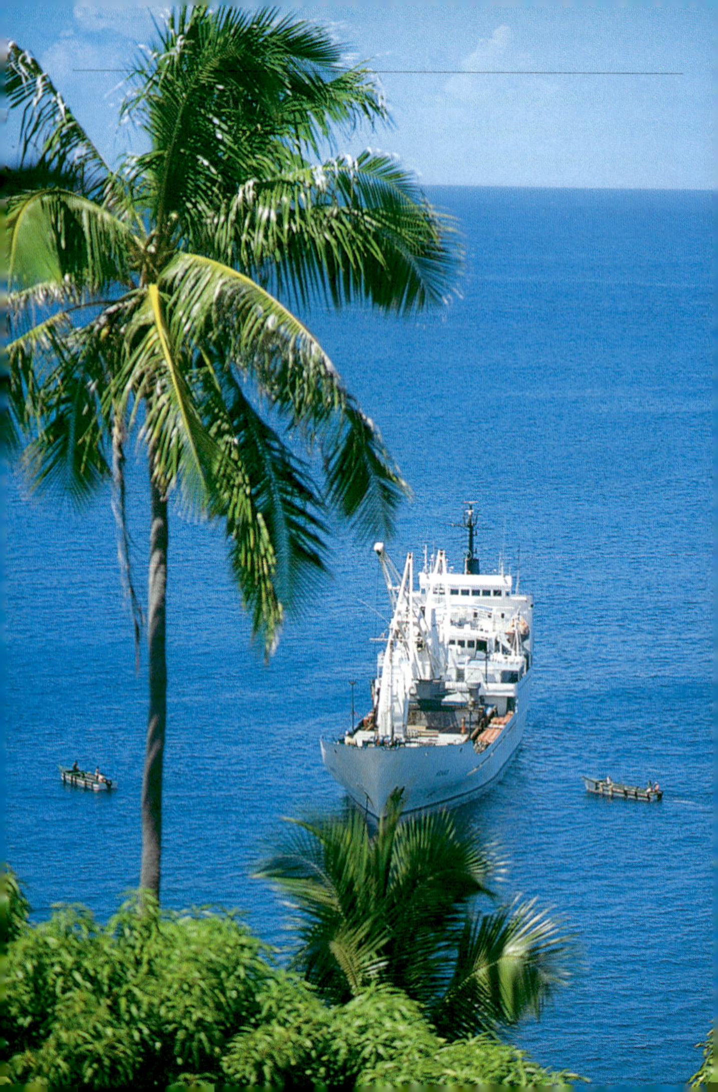

MARQUESAS ISLANDS

Nuku Hiva, Ua Huka, Ua Pou, Hiva Oa, Tahuata, Fatu Hiva

You can't get further away from it all than this. The Marquesas Islands are the most remote pinpoints of land in the world, set in the South Pacific 800 km (500 miles) from their nearest neighbours, the Tuamotu group, and 6,000 km (3,700 miles) from the nearest continent, South America.

Volcanic upheavals thrust up from the ocean these 11 lonely and wildly beautiful islands. Velvety green jungle softens their jagged peaks. Steep valleys lined by groves of bamboo, plantain and coconut plunge down to black sands, edged by clusters of palms. A fringe of white surf rolls in from the east.

Only six islands are inhabited, all with a lazy, tropical lilt to their names: Nuku Hiva, the main island; Hiva Oa, where Paul Gauguin lived; Fatu Hiva, Ua Pou, Ua Huka and Tahuata. According to Marquesan legend, each island of the archipelago was one element of a house: Nuku Hiva the rafters, Ua Pou the columns, Hiva Oa the main roof beam, Fatu Hiva the roof, and so on.

Fifteen times a year, the Aranui *brings a glimpse of the outside world to the Marquesas' villages.*

The Marquesas Islands were the first in French Polynesia to be colonized. The original inhabitants came across the Pacific some 1,600 years ago, perhaps from Samoa, bringing in their large double-hulled craft domestic animals—chickens, pigs and dogs—as well as seedlings to plant in their new homeland, which they named Te Henua Enata, "the land of men". With them came a well-developed Stone Age culture, with the skills to raise giant statues to their gods and to shape fine carvings of wood, tortoiseshell and bone. Slowly conquering the valleys, they founded a strongly hierarchical society centred on religious ceremonies. They fought inter-tribal wars from valley to valley, fiercely tattooed to frighten their enemies, offering human sacrifices to their round-eyed stone deities and indulging in ritual cannibalism.

When the Spanish navigator Mendana landed on Hiva Oa on July 21, 1595, looking for the mythical Solomon Islands, the archipelago had in all probability almost 100,000 inhabitants. He named the islands the Marquesas, in honour of the Marchioness de Mendoza, wife of the viceroy of

Peru. Following an angry skirmish provoked, according to some historians, by the theft of a chandelier, Mendana resorted to the use of firearms. This unfortunate incident was to be the first of many. After the passage of Captain Cook in 1774, it was the turn of the Frenchman Etienne Marchand to call at the islands. In 1791, he took possession of the northern group, but it wasn't until 1842 that French sovereignty was finally imposed on King Iotete by Admiral Dupetit-Thouars. In the wake of the explorers, Europeans came to the islands in increasing numbers—whalers, adventurers of every sort, merchants in quest of sandalwood and missionaries, all bringing with them new ideas and unknown diseases. In 1864 Peruvian slavers took some Marquesans to South America to work in plantations and mines.

Between 1820 and 1916, the population of the Marquesas, already dwindling, fell from 50,000 to 2,000 inhabitants through a combination of tribal wars, dis-

THE ARANUI

Fifteen times a year, the *Aranui*, a 104-m (340-ft) cargo freighter sets out on an unusual voyage to the Marquesas. From Papeete, she heads for the Tuamotu, then sails north to Ua Pou. You can join the ship for the voyage around the Marquesas. Following the itinerary of Herman Melville and Gauguin, the ship plies from port to village, from village to isolated hamlet. At each stop, a few hours long, an amazing variety of cargo is unloaded—cars, refrigerators, washing machines. Sacks and sacks of copra are taken on board, along with a few barrels of *noni* and even on occasion, and with some difficulty, horses. As most of the islands have no quay worth mentioning, you have to reach dry land by jumping into a pitching whaling boat. You can then explore the island on foot, by four-wheel-drive vehicle or on horseback, to discover the features that make the Marquesas archipelago so magical: flower-bedecked villages, sanctuaries, *tikis*, waterfalls, craggy summits, beaches of black sand. In the evenings, heavily tattooed sailors occasionally join in Polynesian chants to the accompaniment of a guitar. Sometimes, they will tempt some of the more audacious tourists to dance in an unrestrained *tamure*.

There are four classes on board ship, ranging from the bridge, where the islanders sleep, to dormitories with bunks, and air-conditioned cabins. It is a unique way of seeing this remote archipelago.

ease and emigration. After Herman Melville, the French writer Pierre Loti (at the time a young midshipman on the *Flore*) and Robert Louis Stevenson lamented the end of a world "in these islands where the number of dead already far exceeds the number of living".

Today the 8,000 Marquesans are staunchly Catholic, and the relics of their ancient temples lie overgrown by jungle. The rich land of the valleys yields breadfruit (the major staple), coffee, vanilla and fruit. The main export is copra. Apart from fishing, the islanders love to go hunting for wild pig, and they are skilled woodcarvers. To get from one valley to the next, they ride on horseback. Their horses are of Chilean stock; brought in by the French in the 19th century, many of them became wild.

Nuku Hiva

The biggest Marquesa has an area of 330 sq km (127 sq miles). Robert Louis Stevenson landed here in 1894 and described it as a "pale phantasmagoria of cliffs and clouds". Formed of several volcanoes, with the highest one, Mount Tekao, rising to 1,185 m (3,888 ft), Nuku Hiva presents a succession of dramatic landscapes of wild beauty: dizzying peaks and lush, narrow valleys forested with slender trees, criss-crossed by footpaths. Around the shoreline, notched by little creeks in the north and wide bays in the south, villages nestle beneath the shade of palms on beaches of black sand. The landing strip at Nuku Ataha on Terre Déserte, the northwest of the island, is a 10-minute helicopter ride or two hours by rough road from the village of Taiohae on the southern coast. The helicopter flight provides a unique opportunity to view the mountain crests cloaked in dark green vegetation, and the high plateau of Toovii.

Taiohae

Lying in a superb protected bay, overlooked by a mountain known as The Sentinel, Taiohae is the principal village of Nuku Hiva and the administrative and economic centre of the archipelago. Until the 1960s, the boats of the merchant marine called here on their way to Sydney. It is still a favourite stopover for trans-Pacific yachtsmen and for visitors who come to see the stone relics of the Marquesan's ancient culture. Beside the sea, the Temeheha *paepae* (stone platform), upon which stand modern *tikis* since the first Marquesan festival in 1987, is still visited by the local notables.Today, they come here to talk politics.

On the other side of the street, the Cathedral of Notre-Dame is the seat of the bishop of the Marquesas. Standing in front of the entrance to the building are two handsome wooden sculptures representing Jesus and St Peter, carved in the traditional decorative style of the Marquesas. Other sculptures in the interior, by craftsmen from every island in the group, illustrate the Stations of the Cross and biblical scenes.

> ### KABRILI I
>
> A Frenchman from Bordeaux, one Joseph Cabris, embarked on a whaler in 1798. The boat capsized off the coast of the Marquesas, but the young man managed to swim ashore. Captured by the natives of Nuku Hiva, he was almost sacrificed. But it was his lucky day: the tribe adopted him and he eventually married the king's daughter. Upon the king's death, he succeeded to the title under the name of Kabrili I. One day, a Russian boat arrived and Kabrili went on board, hoping to obtain the protection of the French government for his kingdom. But in Europe, things didn't run smoothly—both the Tsar and Louis XVIII refused to receive him. Sadly, Kabrili did not have the means to return to the Marquesas. He finished his life in a circus, exhibiting his Marquesan tattoos.

The arrival of the fishing boats on the beach on Saturday mornings is always a lively occasion.

Valleys

From Taiohae you can take trips into the nearby valleys to see numerous *meaes* (equivalent of the Tahitian *marae*) and *tikis*. Hakaui Valley, 15 km (9 miles) to the west, is accessible by boat. Immense cliffs rise on each side, the highest reaching over 800 m (2,600 ft). After a short hike through majestic scenery, you will come upon the Ahuei Falls, among the highest in the world with a drop of 350 m (1,150 ft).

A track from Taiohae climbs up towards Toovii Plateau and the airport, providing several outstanding views over the bay and Ua Pou. At the crest, a fork in the road leads east to the village of Taipivai, nestling at the bottom of a fertile valley of the same name. At the edge of the bay, hemmed by a rim of black sand, rocks form an impressive rampart along the east coast. Herman Melville, who had yet to write *Moby Dick*, made this the setting for his novel *Typee* (1846). Having embarked on the whaler *Acushnet* at the age of 20, Melville jumped ship 18 months later when the boat docked in the Marquesas. He spent three weeks in Taipivai Valley, living with the Taipis, a tribe of cannibals who were at

In the shade of the flame tree, life in Taiohae proceeds at a gentle pace.

war with their neighbours, the Hapaas. Like his hero, he managed to leave the island on board an Australian ship bound for Tahiti. Shortly before arriving, a mutiny broke out on board. Melville took part and as a result arrived in Papeete clapped in irons, before being transferred to the prison of Tipaerui.

Taipivai's carvers work in rosewood. Above the village, you will find an interesting *meae* (thought by some archaeologists to have been the residence of Chief Veahe), with several old stone *tikis* and two *paepaes*. One of them contained a "sacred dustbin", into which everything that had belonged to the chief was thrown—including nail clippings, hair, and so on.

Further north is Hatiheu Valley, where British author Robert Louis Stevenson, lived for a time. Needles of rock, covered with rampant vegetation, overlook the village and its coconut grove at the head of the bay. On one of the summits you can see a white Madonna, set there by the White Fathers.

A 15-minute walk away is the Hikokua *tohua*: the plaza where rituals, including human sacrifices, were performed. Up to 2,000 people used to assemble here for the great ritual ceremonies. It was the custom, before setting out to war, to sacrifice an enemy of inferior rank by stoning him to death. The *tohua* was usually surrounded by the houses of the elders, built of wood on stone platforms (*paepaes*). To one side stood the *meae*, often shaded by the spreading branches of a banyan tree on which were hung the bones of the tribe's heroes. Squat stone *tikis,* with wide mouths and huge eyes, watched over the ceremonies. At Hikokua you'll see an amazing turtle-headed *tiki* (the turtle is the symbol of eternal life).

Nowadays, more peaceful displays of Marquesan dances are given here, including the famous dance of the pig. A little farther up, you can see a few rock carvings—some of which represent turtles—close to a huge banyan tree.

A half-hour's walk will take you to the pass overlooking the sweep of Anaho Bay (it can also be reached by boat). In a sheltered cove, the Marquesas' only beach of pale sand forms a crescent lapped by clear waters and fringed by coconut palms.

Ua Huka

Nuku Hiva's close neighbour Ua Huka is the smallest island of the northern group. Rarely visited and sparsely populated (570 inhabitants), it has a rugged landscape very different from that of the other isles. Its sparsely vegetated hills are home to countless wild horses and goats.

Vaipaee, the main settlement, is hidden at the head of a deep and narrow bay. It has a small museum displaying a collection of Marquesan artefacts (many are replicas of ancient objects) and the reconstruction of a funerary grotto. From here, a track overlooking the sea leads to the Hane Valley. On the way, you can visit an arboretum with a collection of more than 300 tree species from all over the world. Vanilla is also cultivated there.

The most ancient inhabited site of the Marquesas, going back to the 3rd century BC, has been discovered at Hane. In the village, the tiny Museum of the Sea, sharing a building with a craft centre, has two ancient canoes from the Austral Islands and a few model boats. A 20-minute walk will lead you to a small isolated *meae* built on a platform overlooking a coconut grove and Hane Bay. It has three unusual long-eared *tikis* carved out of a red volcanic rock, *keetu*, reserved for nobles' sites. On the way you will probably notice some large holes, where the islanders used to store *popoi*, a fermented paste made from breadfruit.

Off the south coast, Hemeni and Epeti islets are home to a

colony of sooty terns: as many as 200,000 birds breed here every year.

Ua Pou

Its craggy slopes surround the needles of Mount Oave, the highest point in the archipelago at 1,232 m (4,042 ft). As you approach by sea, ranks of cliffs, peaks and jagged outcrops come into view, with a few patches of forest clinging to the heights.

Scarcely 15 km by 10 km (9 miles by 6), the island has 2,000 inhabitants, the second most populous after Nuku Hiva. Its principal village, Hakahau, claims the oldest Christian church in the Marquesas (1859). It contains some fine wooden sculptures and there is a small museum nearby. Anahoa beach can be reached by a 25-minute walk.

The archaeological site of Hakamui Valley ("Valley of the Kings"), once home to the Atipapas tribe, has several *paepaes* and *tikis*. The Mataautea *tiki* is the most interesting. You can hire a horse to explore the steep pathways.

Hiva Oa

Named Dominica by Mendana, who landed here on a Sunday, the "garden of the Marquesas" is the largest and the most fertile of the southern group of islands. Wild horses graze on the slopes of the deep valleys, behind a rampart of high cliffs.

Atuona

Opposite Taaoa Bay (still called Traitors' Bay because in 1816 some islanders seized a merchant vessel there), the principal settlement of Atuona lies in a valley at the foot of the 1,040-m (3,412-ft) Temetiu Peak. Calvary Cemetery, on a hill overlooking the vil-

---

4 THE FOUR BEST BAYS The tormented landscapes of Polynesia have given rise to some of the world's most bewitching bays. The most renowned are **Opunohu Bay** and **Cook's Bay**, both on Moorea. They slice right into the heart of the island like two tropical fjords. Far away in the Marquesas, **Virgins' Bay** on Fatu Hiva, dominating Ilanavave Valley and its coconut groves, is bordered by an imposing rampart of rocky peaks in wildly romantic scenery. On Nuku Hiva, the superb **Taiohae Bay** provides safe anchorage for Pacific yachtsmen.

GAUGUIN

Gauguin was born in France in 1848 but spent his earliest years in Peru. At the age of 17 he joined the merchant navy and sailed around the world. On his return, he took a job with a stockbroking firm and in 1873 married a young Danish woman. He became interested in Impressionist painting and developed a friendship with Pissarro. In 1883, during a financial crisis, he abandoned the stock exchange and decided to devote himself exclusively to painting. Four years later, he took off, leaving behind his wife and five children. He dreamed of reaching Panama, but only got as far as Martinique, where he fell sick and was repatriated the following year. He settled in Brittany and became a leading figure in the Pont-Aven school.

Gauguin sold all his paintings in 1891 and with the proceeds left for Tahiti. In Papeete, he was disappointed to find that the vahines were swathed in austere missionary dresses. He left the town and settled in Mataiea, 45 km (28 miles) away, where he integrated into village life. He threw himself into colour and painted Teha'amana, his Tahitian companion, aged barely 13. He stayed for two years in Mataiea, until the day he found himself penniless. Learning of the death of his uncle, he returned to France to collect his inheritance. But his friends and family weren't interested, and the 80 canvases that were supposed to make his reputation sold badly.

During the summer of 1895 he left again. But on Tahiti, Teha'amana had married, "civilization" had advanced and Gauguin, suffering with syphilis and by now an alcoholic, was in despair. He took flight again, this time to the Marquesas. At Atuona on Hiva Oa island, he built his "House of Pleasure", a simple hut roofed with palm fronds. It was here that he painted his most beautiful works. But he had no personal respite. He fell out with the authorities and the Church, which he accused of wishing to destroy Polynesian culture. His state of health was deplorable and his drinking bouts shocked the authorities, who persecuted him. He was sentenced to three months in prison for defamation of a policeman. While waiting to appeal, he died at his home on May 8, 1903, victim of a heart attack and leaving behind the unfinished *Breton Village under Snow*. Some people still claim that he took his own life. That is not quite the end of the story. The bishop seized 22 canvases and some drawings and burned them in public as the "obscenities of a sad character, enemy of God and all that is honest". Then he gave him a Christian burial.

lage, is the last resting place of Gauguin and of Jacques Brel. Gauguin lies in a simple grave of volcanic rock, shaded by a frangipani tree and watched over by Oviri, a copy in bronze of a terracotta statuette he sculpted in 1894.

The tomb of Jacques Brel, who died in 1978 at the age of 49, is adorned with a medallion representing him with his companion Madly. The Belgian singer, suffering from cancer, decided to end his days here. Walkers may wish to undertake the one-and-a-half-hour climb to the Belvedere, where he had planned to build a house.

In the village, you can visit a reconstruction of Gauguin's "House of Pleasure" on its original site, with its bamboo walls and palm-frond roof. To obtain the land, which belonged to the Church, the painter resolved to attend mass. "I have escaped from everything conventional or artificial", he wrote to his wife in Copenhagen. "I listen to the huge birds suspended in space and I understand the Great Truth."

The neighbouring Segalen-Gauguin Museum bears the name of the friend who discovered the body of the artist. It contains several Marquesan artefacts and copies of Gauguin's works by Alin Marthouret, an ex-forger turned authorized copyist. There is a craft centre on the other side of the road.

To the west, the immense archaeological site of Taaoa groups almost a thousand *paepaes* hidden beneath the vegetation and sheltered by the arching branches of *mapes*, with a large *tohua* and a *meae* adorned by a big-eared *tiki*, similar to those found on Ua Huka.

Puamau Valley

From Atuona, you can get to Puamau Valley on the northeast coast by boat (90 min) or on foot along a winding track (3 h). Half-an-hour's walk from the village, the largest archaeological site in French Polynesia lies in the middle of the jungle. This ancient residence of a great chief of the Naiki tribe, restored in 1991, was transformed into a *meae* in 1880 after the tribe had been wiped out by their enemies, the Tio'u. It includes a huge *tiki*, 2.5 m (8 ft) tall, representing Chief Takaii. In the background, another *tiki* depicts a woman kneeling in labour. You will notice that both figures have very large heads: the head was *tapu* (and thought to radiate supernatural power) in Mahoi mythology. The most surprising *tiki* of all is nevertheless the figure of a woman lying on her stomach, Maki Tana Pepe. A rock carving on its side has given rise to a controversy. The Norwe-

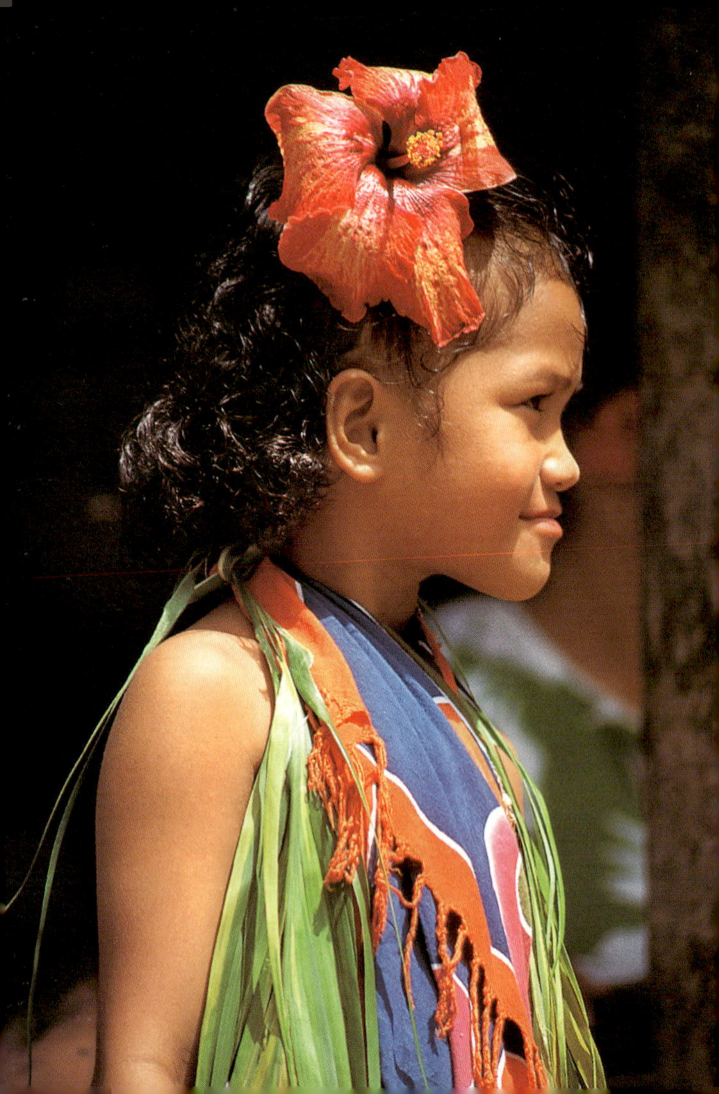

gian anthropologist Thor Heyerdahl was convinced that it represented a lama, supporting his theory that Polynesia was populated from South America. Others see a dog—or the representation of the woman's children.

Below, in the direction of the grey sandy beach, the tomb of Tehau Moena, the last tribal queen of the valley, is located on private property (ask for permission if you want to see it). They say she was buried with her bicycle because she couldn't bear to be parted from it.

Tahuata

Separated from Hiva Oa by the Bordelais Channel, Tahuata is the smallest of the Marquesas' inhabited islands, with a population of 640. The main settlement is Vaitahu, in the shade of coconut palms and breadfruit trees. It was at Vaitahu Bay that Mendana disembarked in 1595, and here that the first confrontation with the islanders took place. It is also the spot where the first horses arrived in 1842, sent from Chile and presented by Admiral Dupetit-Thouars to King Iotete after he had obtained recognition of French sovereignty. The octagonal Catholic church of Vaitahu was inaugurated in 1988 to mark the 150th anniversary of the landing of the first missionaries on the Marquesas. It has an amazing modern stained-glass window showing the Virgin and Child, with Mary in missionary dress surrounded by breadfruit trees. Display cases in the town hall contain archaeological items discovered on the island.

A two-hour walk along the coast leads to the village of Hapatoni, wedged at the foot of the cliffs. In the other direction at the northwest point, lies the pale sandy beach of Hanamoenoa.

KON-TIKI EXPEDITION

Thor Heyerdahl stayed on Fatu Hiva in 1936 and studied the population and fauna. Struck by the resemblance between some of the island's *tikis* and the gigantic monoliths of pre-Inca civilizations, he surmised that Polynesia had been populated from South America.

In 1948, to prove his theory, he left Peru with five companions on board a simple raft of balsa wood. Borne across the ocean by the currents, the team covered 6,500 km (4,000 miles) and landed on the reef of Raroia, in the southwest of the Marquesas, after a voyage of 101 days. All of which, incidentally, proved nothing.

A budding Polynesian beauty.

Fountain of youth, aspirin of the Ancients—the noni *could be the latest miracle cure.*

Fatu Hiva

The most southerly of the Marquesas Islands is formed by two interlocking volcanoes riddled with gorges and ravines. Wetter and greener than the others, the island is spectacular. Its 630 inhabitants are shared between two villages. Most live in Omoa in the southwest, where the pointed church steeple and the neat rows of canoes are hidden from view beneath stands of coconut palms.

Do not miss the small museum set up by the local chief in a house behind the church. It contains some magnificent ancient Marquesan artefacts: weapons such as clubs and spears, *otue* (containers to hold the head of a dead person and placed in a funerary grotto), and more.

A four- or five-hour hike along a path meandering through pandanus and mango forest takes you to the village of Hanavave, 17 km (10 miles) away. It is tucked away in the famous Baie des Vierges, often described as the most beautiful in all the Pacific. The original name given by visiting sailors was *Baie des Verges*, "Penis Bay"—after the phallic shape of the enormous rocks guarding the valley. When the missionaries arrived they inserted an "i", to change it into the less offensive "Virgins' Bay". From the sea, the only traces of civilization are a white chapel and one small house.

Long reputed for producing the most intricate tattoo designs in Polynesia, the island is the last one where *tapa* fabric is still made in the traditional manner. The cloth is made from the bark of trees, beaten until the fibres are supple.

Another product of the island is a perfumed oil, *monoi umu hei*, supposed to have seductive powers. It is composed of coconut oil and *tiare*, together with sandalwood, mint, jasmine, ginger root, pineapple, basil and other exotic ingredients.

> **NONI**
>
> Traditionally used by Polynesians as a panacea, the nasty-tasting *noni* fruit has recently attracted the interest of modern medicine. Preliminary studies seem to indicate that it could be effective in the treatment of cancer, and it is already on sale in the United States as an appetite suppressant. In the Marquesas, an increasing number of copra producers are turning to the cultivation of *noni*: each tree can yield more than 20 kg (44 lb) of fruit per harvest, the work is much less demanding and just as lucrative.

5 THE FIVE MOST IMPRESSIVE MARAES The ancient Polynesians left their temples open to the elements, and in some of them, the *tikis* they worshipped still stand. At **Arahurahu** on Tahiti, *tikis* watch over the sites where ancient ceremonies are re-enacted during the July festivities. On Huahine, the chiefs lived in the village of **Maeva**, where you can still see dozens of private and public *maraes* around the superb communal house, *fare pote'e*. Raiatea was the religious and political centre of the islands, and travellers from all over Polynesia assembled there at the **Taputapuatea** *marae*. To admire the tallest *tikis* in Polynesia, you must go to the Marquesas, more specifically to the **Puamau** *marae* on Hiva Oa island. The immense stone platforms (*paepaes*) in **Hatiheu Valley** on Nuku Hiva contain some fine sculptures. Nowadays, displays of Marquesan dances are given here.

CULTURAL NOTES

Dance

Traditional Tahitian dancing was banned for many years because 19th-century European missionaries judged it futile and indecent. However, the dances were still practised in secret and have gradually resurfaced with the revival of Polynesian cultural awareness and as tourists began to show their appreciation for this type of entertainment. The vahines' hip-gyrating *tamure* is the most familiar, but it dates in fact only from the 1950s (its name comes from a contemporary song).

The men specialize in war dances, or fire dances in which they juggle with flaming torches. Partly preserved in the Marquesas, the old dance themes were closely linked to daily life and ceremony; the best known is the dance of the pig.

Musical accompaniment is provided by the ukulele, which has now replaced the *vivo* (a bamboo nose flute) and the *pu* (a shell blown to announce the start of the ceremonies). The ancient drums are still sometimes played—the great *pahu* (formerly made from a stretched shark skin) or the *to'ere* (a hollowed tree trunk).

Canoes

The most typical boat of Polynesia is the outrigger canoe *(va'a)*. But when the ancient voyagers conquered the Pacific, they sailed in much larger vessels. The ocean-going *pahi*, no longer used, was a twin-hulled canoe with sails of plaited pandanus, similar in shape to modern catamarans and well-suited for fishing, travelling or going to war. Built under the protection of the gods, they were launched with due religious ceremony. An 18th-century navigator described a *pahi* he saw near Fiji: 36 m (118 ft) long and with a mast 24 m (79 ft) high. During ocean crossings, coconuts, pigs, chickens and dogs were taken along as food.

The Polynesians were skilled navigators, tracing their course by the movements of the sun, the stars, the moon and the winds. At night, they relied on more than 120 stars and planets to estimate their latitude and direction. During the daytime, they could interpret signs in the sky: a greenish reflection on the underside of a cloud, for example, could reveal the presence of an otherwise invisible atoll up to 40 km (25 miles) away. Captain Cook recognized their knowledge and was pleased to take aboard a Maohi in Tahiti, who helped him chart many of the neighbouring islands.

In 1976, a navigator from Micronesia decided to retrace the route taken by Polynesians who set off from the Marquesas to colonize Hawaii in the 6th century. His voyage of 4,000 km (2,500 miles) across the ocean on board the *Hokule'a*, a reconstruction of an ancient canoe, has been the inspiration for many others.

Marae

In the ancient Polynesian world, everything was pervaded by the notion of the sacred—from the basic elements of daily life to political and social structures. The *marae* was a religious site where the ancestors or the gods could be invoked, but it was also an expression of social status and family organization.

Consequently, there were different types of *marae*. Private ancestral *maraes* were reserved for each family, while corporations of sculptors, sorcerers, tattooists, and so on, also had their own. Among the public *maraes*, Taputapuatea on Raiatea was the only one of international significance, being a centre of political and religious assembly for several Pacific archipelagos. The district chiefs, *ari'i*, embodying spiritual and temporal power, each had a *marae* dedicated to Oro, the god of war. Here, human sacrifices and the various rituals of social life were practised.

Taboo

Of Polynesian origin, *tapu* is often used today merely to indicate private property, but traditionally it was a means of prohibiting access to a sacred site. When a place was declared *tapu*, no one would enter on pain of death until it was lifted. Taboos could thus be short or long-term, and even today, people resort to sorcerers to remove evil spells from many *tapu* sites. Some people still refuse to enter the ruins of a *marae*. No one would dare remove so much as a pebble or, even worse, a *tiki*. These stone statues (or the smaller wooden *ti'i*) serve as intermediaries between men and the gods and represent deified ancestors—great chiefs, warrior heroes and priests. Some of the *tikis* are still imbued with *mana*, a vital force that permeates every living creature and every object. Anyone who offends them is likely to suffer dire consequences: illness, bad luck or even death. But a well-treated *tiki* can give protection against misfortune. The *mana* is unstable and may disappear with time. To keep on the safe side, remember that "dead" *tikis* are still covered in moss.

Tupapau, ghosts or spirits of the dead, are often considered to be malevolent. They generally venture out under cover of darkness. For this reason, Polynesians do not like moonless nights and will often leave a light burning from dusk till dawn to keep the spirits away.

Tapa

The only island producing barkcloth in French Polynesia is Fatu Hiva in the Marquesas; it is also made in Fiji and Tonga. The inner bark of three different tree species

Cultural Notes

is used: the *eute* or *aute* (paper mulberry) gives a very white *tapa*, previously reserved for chiefs; the *mei* (breadfruit tree) gives a light beige *tapa* worn by persons of inferior rank; the *aoa* or *ora* (banyan) produces a dark brown *tapa* which is virtually waterproof. To make the cloth, the bark is split from the tree where it is thinnest and then peeled from the wood. The soft inner layer is then stripped from the hard outer bark, soaked in water then beaten for several hours with a square mallet of ironwood, *aito*. By the end of the process, the strips of bark have spread to several times their initial size. They are sewn together to make a length of cloth and then decorated.

Tattooing

Developed as an instrument of war to intimidate the enemy, tattooing was customary all over Polynesia, but the technique was perfected especially in the Marquesas and in New Zealand. It also represented a rite of passage into adulthood for young men between the ages of 15 and 20, for whom the ability to bear the pain was a proof of maturity. The dye was made from soot obtained by burning the fruit of the candlenut tree, and was applied using a sharpened bird's bone or shark's tooth, hit with a mallet to puncture the skin. Sessions could last many days. The patterns represented a sort of "clothing", designed to avoid competition with the gods, who enjoyed the privilege of nudity. As he grew older, each man would have new, codified designs added to various parts of his body. The patterns changed according to the whims of fashion, but in the end, they summarized the history of his life.

Women were tattooed at an earlier age and only on the lips, behind the ears, on the limbs and fingers. When someone died, the lines drawn during life had to be scraped off to allow the soul to leave the body. Nowadays, the custom of tattooing has been revived and reinforces the feeling of cultural belonging.

Tiare and Other Flowers

The *Gardenia tahitensis* is the flower truly native to Polynesia. All the other common species—hibiscus, parrot's beak, bird of paradise—were imported, initially by the Polynesians themselves and then by European explorers. The *tiare* flower is used in the production of Tahiti's most famous export, *monoi*. This "perfumed oil" was used as a panacea, for perfuming the body and for anointing the bodies of dead kings. The women, who used to cover their children with it, still use the oil to take care of their skin and their hair.

Tahitian women often wear a flower behind one ear. Behind the left, it means they are married. Behind the right, they are single and looking for a husband.

Shopping

Tahiti offers varied shopping possibilities, but the best souvenirs are handicrafts, especially sculpture and basket weaving. The cost of living is high so you're not likely to find any bargains. Don't try to haggle: the practice is seriously considered taboo. To get an idea of price and quality, look round the covered markets at Papeete or Pirae, 10 minutes to the east and well known for its fine craftsmanship.

Basketwork

Basket-weaving is a popular craft all over French Polynesia, and more specifically in the Austral Islands. Raw materials are mainly dried pandanus leaves, but also young leaves of the coconut palm or the local bamboo. They make straw hats (worn for the Sunday church service), handbags and shopping baskets, cigarette cases, fans, and so on.

Cosmetics

Exported all over the world, *monoi* is coconut oil perfumed with fragrant *tiare* flowers, and sometimes with sandalwood or vanilla. Incorporated into soap and a wide range of lotions and creams, it can be used to help you tan more quickly (be careful if you have a sensitive skin), to add shine to your hair, or as a massage oil.

Another oil, the yellow-green *tamanu*, is harvested from the fruit of the *ati* tree. It is used to protect the hair and skin from the sun and as a moisturizer.

Food, Fruit and Flowers

Tahaa in the Society Islands and the Marquesas are good places for stocking up on vanilla pods. Also in the Marquesas you will find dried bananas and delicious black banyan honey. On Moorea, alcoholic liqueurs are produced from exotic fruit.

Some last-minute airport buys: a carton containing two fresh pineapples, and a long-lasting bouquet of bird-of-paradise or of anthuriums, specially packed for travelling.

Pearls

The famous black pearls of infinitely varied shades can be bought individually or mounted, either from jewellers on Tahiti or directly from the producers in the Tuamotu islands. All Polynesian women wear them in necklaces, bracelets and rings, set off to their best advantage in gold. They are not exactly cheap but certainly the most desirable of all Tahitian souvenirs. If you succumb to temptation, take great care of your pearls, and protect them from damp, perfume and aerosol sprays. However, they should be washed regularly and wiped occasionally with olive oil.

You'll also see jewellery made of shells or mother-of-pearl (pendants, earrings, etc.), sometimes skilfully engraved.

Textiles

The most useful holiday garment for women is the pareo, which can be worn as a skirt with a T-shirt, a cover-up on the beach, or just used to sit on. You'll notice that the women of each island tie their pareos in different ways. Try and get hold of the brochure explaining the 16 ways of wrapping and knotting them. The lengths of fabric are often hand-painted with brightly coloured patterns or images of exotic fish and birds, or with reproductions of Gauguin's paintings.

For men, there are plenty of boutiques selling colourful Tahitian shirts patterned with hibiscus or ginger flowers.

In the 19th century, the wives of Protestant clergymen coming from New England taught the Tahitian women a style of patchwork known here as *tifaifai*. The craft has been handed down to the present day, and you will find cushion covers or quilts made either by patiently stitching together small pieces of fabric or by sewing a mosaic of shapes onto a background. The designs can be abstract, represent flowers or animals, or depict scenes of Tahitian life.

Tapa cloth from the Marquesas Islands was once used for clothing or as a wall divider but today is simply decorative. However, it is sometimes made into hats or even postcards.

Woodcarving and Replicas

The traditional Maohi craft of woodcarving is practised in the Marquesas and to a lesser extent in the Austral Islands. You'll see some magnificent reproductions of ancient objects: war clubs and spears, daggers with carved handles, musical instruments (ukuleles and the great *pahu* or *to'ere* drums), delicate bracelets and hairpins carved from rosewood *(miro)* or fragrant sandalwood *(tou)*, rare nowadays. Cooking utensils are very appealing, and *umete,* dishes made from various fruitwoods and used for fermenting *popoi*. Other souvenirs include little stone *tikis*, carved coconut shells and copies of ancient whale hooks.

Dining Out

Polynesian cuisine is prepared essentially from fresh local produce. Its exotic ingredients blend happily with a good pinch of French knowhow and a dash of Chinese cooking. Fish features prominently on the menu; the islanders prefer it raw but don't worry, they'll cook it for you. However, the most traditional Tahitian meal is the banquet, called the tamara'a. A large pit, ahima'a, is dug in the ground, and into it go a suckling pig and various fish and vegetables wrapped in banana leaves, placed on a bed of red-hot stones, covered with earth and left to braise slowly for at least four hours. On a practical note, bear in mind that service can be very slow and that there is no point in getting impatient.

Breakfast
A traditional breakfast is still prepared in some homes on Sunday mornings. It is a veritable feast, the menu including raw clams and roast pork, prepared the previous evening or early in the morning.

More usual fare is fish, raw or fried. You may prefer coconut bread or doughnuts, *frifri*.

Appetizers
Once you have tasted it you'll get addicted to *poisson cru* (raw fish). Cut into small cubes, sprinkled with lemon juice and coconut milk, fresh tuna or sometimes bonito is served all day long, spiced up with garlic and chives, grated carrot, chopped onion and tomato. It is full of flavour. Salads are also served as starters, as are cocktails of freshwater shrimp, *chevrettes*, embellished with fruit such as coconut or mango.

Fish
Out of the lagoon and into the embers, fish are simply grilled or cooked wrapped in leaves. They may be served with *sauce corail* (made with the red coral of scallops), *sauce américaine* (incorporating tomatoes and cognac), melted butter, or just a splash of lemon juice. The king of fish is the *mahi mahi* (often pronounced "meh meh"). It is the delicately flavoured porgie, a member of the sea bass family. Fresh tuna is a feast, whether it is served in thin,

Dining Out

Fish are washed by the tides into traps on the coral reef.

raw slices Japanese-fashion *(sashimi)* or as a thick and juicy steak. Also much appreciated are parrotfish and kingfish *(tazard)*. Bonito has a more pronounced flavour, and swordfish is delicious when served raw, thinly sliced and marinated in dill and lemon. It can be a bit tough when grilled, and Tahitians don't normally eat it. Nor do they care for shark, which they don't even bother to catch. On the other hand, they are extremely fond of the little shrimp, *chevrettes*, often eaten curried.

The seafood is first-class, particularly sautéed crab, grilled spiny lobster and the local oysters, which are becoming a rarity. Clams *(pahua)* may be curried, or stewed with ham and shrimps. The Tahitians prefer them the minute they are caught, with a squeeze of lemon juice. They also like black sea-urchins, the same way. *Varo* is a sort of scampi, rare but absolutely delicious.

Meat and Vegetables

Perhaps surprisingly, Polynesians are great meat-eaters. Beef often features on the menu in Tahiti—less frequently on the other islands—as does lamb imported from New Zealand. Pork and chicken are more traditional. Pork is wrapped in banana leaves and baked in an earth oven. Lemon chicken, and *fafa* (chicken with taro leaves) are quite good, as is the unusual duck breast with papaya. Kebabs are often seasoned with ginger and coconut.

When the American GIs occupied Bora Bora during World War II, the Polynesians acquired a taste for tinned corned beef. They like it hot, and usually serve it with grilled *uru* (also called *maiore*)—breadfruit, the equivalent of our potato.

In the Marquesas, breadfruit is the base of *popoi*, a fermented paste which is sometimes stored for months at a time in holes dug in the ground.

Among the more unfamiliar Polynesian vegetables, there is *taro*, a starchy tuber which is cooked in the same way as potatoes, roasted or boiled. Its leaves are also edible and when cooked resemble cabbage or spinach. Red, sweet bananas are also prepared as vegetables, as well as their relative, the more starchy, less sweet plantain, *fei*. The sweet potato, or yam, somehow found its way to Polynesia from Central America.

Desserts

In Polynesian restaurants, the dessert trolley arrives groaning with delectable French pastries—cream-filled choux, éclairs, open fruit tarts, gâteaux, and so on—not forgetting caramel custard, coconut cream and classic soufflés. The tropical fruit is bigger, sweeter and juicier than you ever imagined: pineapples, mangoes, papayas, guavas, litchis, melons, giant grapefruit, made into fruit salads or incorporated into cakes. Rum-flavoured pineapple cake is quite popular.

But the Tahitian's favourite dessert, *poe,* rarely appears on restaurant menus. Made from cassava flour, it is nothing other than your familiar, old-fashioned tapioca pudding, enhanced with fruit (banana, papaya or mango) and sometimes covered with a coconut sauce.

Drinks

Most French mineral waters, beers and wines are available, though the prices are higher than in Europe. Hinano, the locally brewed beer is a good, light lager. In some of the Marquesas, small quantities of pineapple or orange beer are brewed for private consumption.

The fresh fruit juices are excellent, especially pineapple, but also papaya and corossol, which tastes something like strawberry. There's nothing more refreshing than coconut milk, fresh from the shell.

Coffee is served strong, black or with milk, and often delicately perfumed with vanilla.

Sports

Polynesia is paradise for those who love the sea. Sheltered deep-water lagoons are dream locations for swimming, diving, big-game fishing and all other water sports. The average water temperature is 26°C (79°F) in the dry season and 29°C (84°F) during the European winter. Add to the list of possibilities yacht or catamaran cruises, and on dry land, excursions on foot or on horseback, golf (on Tahiti), tennis and even paragliding on Nuku Hiva and Tubuai.

Diving

For diving enthusiasts, Polynesian waters are among the best in the world. More than 350 species of fish live around the coral reefs, including the Napoleon fish, the Picasso trigger fish, the balloon fish, which fills itself with water when threatened, and the toad fish, which grunts like a toad when disturbed.

The atolls of the Tuamotu, Rangiroa, Manihi, Tikehau, and many more, promise memorable diving. The presence of sharks adds a little spice to the experience. They are easy to spot: black-tipped reef sharks tend to congregate at the entrance to the passes between the reefs. In some places, the instructors toss them chunks of fish, and several dozen home in at once to tear it apart with their sharp little teeth. You may also see hammerhead sharks and schools of dolphins. Giant manta rays keep themselves to the outer reef; large numbers gather in September and October.

The Society Islands also have fabulous diving sites. You can charter a boat to take you to the best areas. Around Bora Bora, even beginners can hope to spot mantas gliding beneath the waves in a silent ballet, and see Moray eels and giant barracuda. Troops of grey and black-tipped reef sharks patrol the east coast of Raiatea, near the Iriru Channel, and the coral in this area has unchanging colours. You can explore the wreck of a three-master sunk in 1914.

Moorea is less highly rated but has amazing coral "rose gardens", and you can safely swim close to large lemon sharks. It is also worth seeing the Huahine passes, and Tahaa's spectacular

SPORTS

purple and yellow coral. More intrepid divers will enjoy the thrills of diving by night.

Water Sports

Top of the list comes surfing, the great favourite of young Polynesians who practically climb onto their surfboards before they can even toddle. You'll find the best waves at the approaches to the passes in the reef.

Windsurfers can practise their sport almost anywhere. The winds are stronger in places like the Martin *motu* near Point Venus on Tahiti. Most of the big hotels can provide all the necessary equipment. You can also go waterskiing and hire jet skis.

Fully equipped deep-sea boats can be chartered for half- or full-day game fishing expeditions, and excitement is guaranteed. The catch is likely to include marlin, swordfish, tuna or *mahi mahi*. Or you can join the local fishermen with their dragnets in the lagoon.

Hiking

The best island for hiking is Tahiti, especially inland around Mounts Orohena, Diadème and Aorai, which has a shelter at 1,798 m (5,900 ft). Get in touch with the Tahiti Alpine Club (tel. 18 10 59) for its excursion programme. The most beautiful hike takes you round the southern point of Tahiti Iti in a superb jungle landscape, where isolated valley unfurl as you advance, revealing archaeological sites. In places the track clings to dizzying cliffs and some parts are extremely difficult to pass. You will need a guide.

From Mahina, near Venus Point (departure point PK10.2), you can follow the Tuauru river bed to the Faufiru and Tuauru falls (in places, you'll get your feet wet). Moorea, Raiatea and Bora Bora are also ideal for exploration along half-forgotten paths that can be troublesome to follow without local help.

Even experienced hikers will find the Marquesas something of a challenge. The 17-km (10-mile) trek from Omoa to the Baie des Vierges on Fatu Hiva is now considered a classic.

Riding

The best way to explore the more out-of-the-way islands, such as the Marquesas and the Australs, is on horseback. Your mount will carry you into remote valleys where you can discover archaeological sites and *tikis*. Treks of several days, crossing Nuku Hiva, for example, are possible. There are several equestrian clubs in the Society Islands, and it's easy to arrange rides—along Bora Bora's Tofari *motu*, on Huahine, Raiatea, and so on.

The Hard Facts

To help you plan your trip, here is some useful information about French Polynesia.

Airports

The airport at Bora Bora, built by American GIs in World War II, was for a long time the only one in French Polynesia. From there, you had to take a hydroplane to get to Tahiti. Today, flights land at the international airport of Faaa, 5 km (3 miles) west of Papeete. Facilities include a bank, bureau de change, car-hire agencies, post office and duty-free shop. Light refreshments are available and there is a 24-hour information desk.

On Bora Bora, a free shuttle service leaves Motu Mute, the site of the airstrip, 20 minutes after flights land, and takes you to Vaitape in 25 minutes. For the return trip, leave Vaitape 1½ hours before your flight departure. You have to pay for transfers to Maupiti and Nuku Hiva, where you have the choice of a 10-minute helicopter flight or a 2-hour ride in a four-wheel drive vehicle between the airport and Taiohae.

Note that the weight of your luggage will be strictly controlled on Air Tahiti flights—maximum 20 kg (44 lb) for international passengers, and 10 kg (22 lb) if you have spent more than a week on Tahiti.

Climate

French Polynesia enjoys a tropical climate, hotter and wetter from the end of November to the end of March (28–32°C, 82–90°F). This is described as the hot season. The best time for a holiday is between mid-April and mid-October, more particularly from July to September, when the *maaramu*, a southeasterly breeze, is blowing. The average temperature is then 24°C (75°F)—except in the Austral Islands where it is cooler.

The climate in the Marquesas, closer to the equator, is more humid. The rains come later there, too.

Cyclones are relatively rare compared with the rest of the South Pacific. They are principally active between November and March and become increasingly frequent the closer you get to the Tropic of Capricorn. In recent years, the El Niño current has caused some exceptional disturbances, as in many other parts of the world.

Clothing
Whatever the season, have your swimsuit, your sunglasses and a sunhat close at hand. Light cotton clothing is the most suitable. For ladies, a pareo will prove invaluable. Plastic sandals are useful for swimming: in many places the sand gives way suddenly to coral. These are readily and cheaply available on the spot.

Communications
The length of time for the post to reach its destination varies considerably. It all depends where you post your mail, and a pinch of good luck. In general, allow 4 to 10 days for Europe and North America.

To make an international phone call, dial 00 and the country code (1 for US and Canada, 44 for UK), the area code (omitting the initial 0), and the local number. All public telephone boxes operate with a phone card specific to Polynesia (many of which are prized by collectors). National calls are cheap; international calls are getting cheaper all the time, with reduced rates between midnight and 6 a.m. The country code for calling Polynesia from abroad is 689; local numbers have six figures.

Faxes can be sent from the main post office on Papeete and from most hotels.

Customs and Formalities
A valid passport and a return air ticket are required in principle for all EU citizens. Nationals of other countries may need a visa. As requirements are subject to change, it is best to get in touch with the consulate or consular section of your nearest French embassy for up-to-date information before finalizing your travel arrangements.

Travellers aged 17 years and over may import the following goods without incurring customs duty: 200 cigarettes or 50 cigars or 250 g tobacco; 2 litres of spirits over 22° or 1 litre of spirits over 22° and 2 litres still wine; 50 g perfume and 250 ml eau de toilette; goods up to a value of 5000 CFP francs.

Driving
To hire a car, you generally need to be over 21 years of age and to have held a licence for at least one year.

Within the Society Islands, the coastal roads are in good condition. Most are tarmacked and those that are not are nevertheless suitable for hired vehicles. The speed limit is generally 60 kph (37 mph) out of town and 40 kph (25 mph) in built-up areas. On the

The Hard Facts

dual carriageway near Papeete, the limit is 90 kph (55 mph). When driving at night, look out for pedestrians, cyclists without lights and animals crossing the road.

In the Tuamotu, people get around by boat. In the Marquesas, most visitors leave it to local drivers to negotiate the difficult and muddy tracks, or hire a horse.

Electricity
All the islands are supplied with electricity—the smallest by generator. Although in some old hotels the supply is still 110 volts, the norm is now 220 volts AC, 60 Hz. American-style 2-pin plugs are used.

Health
Risks to health are minimal. There are no snakes, poisonous or otherwise in Polynesia. The sting of the *nono*, a gnat commonly found on the atolls (and in the Marquesas), is extremely itchy. A mosquito repellent will come in useful but, alas, has no effect on the *nono*. The Polynesians find that *monoi* helps, as long as you apply plenty of it. Watch out also for centipedes, some as long as 10 cm (4 inches) and with a painful sting.

When you swim in lagoons, you should be more wary of the coral than of sharks (very few serious accidents have occurred since records began). Cuts inflicted by sharp coral can be slow to heal if they are not disinfected. You should also beware of the sting of the stonefish, very difficult to see because it is well camouflaged on the seabed. Watch out for certain molluscs—the sting of cone shells can be fatal.

Otherwise, your only enemy will be the sun. You will need a sun cream with a high protection factor; it will not stop you getting a tan, but will prevent painful burns if you renew the applications properly. Wear sunglasses by the sea to reduce glare and, if possible, a hat. During the heat of the day, some people swim in their T-shirts.

Holidays and Festivals
January 1	New Year
May 1	Labour Day
July 14	Bastille Day
August 15	Assumption
September 8	Internal Autonomy Day
November 1	All Saints' Day
November 11	Armistice Day, *Hawaiki nui va'a* (canoe race)
December 25	Christmas Day

Moveable:
Jan or Feb	Chinese New Year
Early March	Missionary Day
March or April	Good Friday
	Easter Monday

THE HARD FACTS

May or June	Ascension Day Whit Monday

There are also several competitions and festivals:

March	International surfing competition
April	Maohi Sports Day: javelin, stone-lifting competitions, etc.
July	*Heiva i Tahiti,* from June 29, the Anniversary of Internal Autonomy, to the beginning of August.
September	Tahiti Flower Show
end Oct.	Carnival
mid-Nov.	Stone fishing on Bora Bora and Moorea
Beg. Dec.	Tiare Days

Language

The official languages are Tahitian and French, which is spoken by virtually everyone, rolling the "r". English is widely understood by islanders used to meeting foreign visitors. The language of the Marquesas is quite different from Tahitian.

In the melodious Tahitian language, vowels play an extremely important role. Consonants are always separated by at least one vowel, and every word ends with a vowel. When a word has several vowels together, they are generally pronounced separately, although some diphthongs do exist. The apostrophe is used to indicate a pause in the pronunciation (for example, *popa'a* or *he'i*), but it is often omitted. The Tahitian alphabet has only 13 letters, comprising five vowels, *a* (as in "cat"), *e* ("ay"), *i* ("ee"), *o* (as in "cold") and *u* (pronounced "oo") and eight consonants: f, h, m, n, p, r, t and v.

Here are a few words you'll find easy to remember:

aita	no
aita pea pea	never mind, it doesn't matter
e	yes
fenua	Polynesian people or land
fiu	fed up
ia orana	good morning, good day
maeva	welcome
maitai	good
maururu	thank you
nana	goodbye
tamaa	to eat
tatau	tattoo
tane	man
vahine	woman

Media

Two daily papers (both in French), *La Dépêche de Tahiti* and the *Nouvelles de Tahiti*, serve the Polynesian readership. There is an English-language weekly, *Tahiti Beach Press*.

The local television has only three channels, RFO1, RFO2 and

Canal Plus Polynésie. The French television news is broadcast at 8 a.m. (TF1), noon (France 2) and in the evening (France 3). Most of the big hotels offer cable TV with programmes in English.

The most popular radio stations are Radio Maohi (the government station) and Radio Tefana (independent).

Money Matters

Banking hours in the Society Islands are Monday to Friday 8 a.m.–3.30 p.m. (restricted hours in the other archipelagos).

Exchange facilities are available at the airport, in major banks, and at authorized hotels and shops in Papeete. No commission is charged for changing cash, or for cashing travellers cheques in US dollars (or French francs). There are plenty of automatic cash distributors in Papeete. The major credit cards, especially American Express, are widely accepted in the Society Islands; elsewhere their use is more limited and you should make sure you have sufficient cash.

French Polynesia is part of the French Monetary Area. The unit of currency is the CFP (French Pacific Community) franc. Coins are issued in denominations of 1, 2, 5, 10, 20, 50 and 100 CFP francs; banknotes in denominations of 500, 1000, 5000 and 10,000 CFP francs.

Opening Hours

Business hours are generally Monday to Friday 8 a.m.–noon and 1.30–5.30 p.m. Shops open Monday to Friday 7.30 a.m.–5 p.m. and Saturday 7.30 a.m.–11 a.m. They sometimes close for lunch, anywhere between 11 a.m. and 2 p.m. Shopping centres in Papeete's suburbs may stay open until 8 p.m. Everything is closed on Sundays, apart from Chinese shops which open in the morning.

Museums are closed on Mondays and public holidays.

Photography

Take enough film and video cassettes with you when you leave home, as these are much more expensive to buy on the spot. Slow film (25 to 100 ASA) is recommended for use in the dazzling light conditions. A polarizing filter is very useful during the hottest hours of the day and will bring out the greens of the lagoon and the yellows of the coconut palms. The people are usually willing to pose for photographs provided you ask them politely.

Safety

Since the end of nuclear testing, unemployment has increased and with it the inevitable consequences. Theft is more common than previously, especially in Papeete. The golden rule is never to leave anything in your car.

THE HARD FACTS

Certain areas of the capital, frequented by sailors, should be avoided at night.

On the outer islands, there is in general no problem. Nevertheless, do not put temptation in anyone's way and leave your valuables in the hotel safe.

Time
In Tahiti and the Society Islands, the Tuamotu archipelago and the Austral Islands, the time, year-round, is GMT –10. In the Gambier Islands it is GMT –9 and in the Marquesas GMT –9.5.

Tipping
In general tipping is not practised as it considered contrary to the Tahitian idea of hospitality. However, it is tolerated in establishments frequented by foreigners.

Transport
Air Tahiti runs regular domestic flights to all the archipelagos of the territory, no matter how remote. There's a 10-minute shuttle between Papeete and Moorea once or twice an hour. It's well worth investing in a special air pass which offers flights to several islands within 28 days, for a fixed price.

Ferries, catamarans, copra boats and schooners make regular trips through the islands. They are the preferred means of transport of the Polynesians and in fact the only means of reaching certain islands. It's much cheaper than flying, but you have to put up with frequent delays. There are daily connections between Papeete, Moorea, Huahine, Raiatea and Bora Bora. The Marquesas and Austral islands are served once a fortnight, and Mangareva, in the Gambiers, once a month.

Locally, if you have not rented a car, then you travel by "truck", a wooden-sided lorry converted into a bus. They leave from the central market in Papeete town centre and travel to all the villages. There is no timetable, but scheduled stops are indicated by blue signs. Just wave your hand and the driver will stop to pick you up. You pay when you get off.

Taxis are available in Tahiti, Moorea, Bora Bora, Huahine and Raiatea, but they are very expensive.

INDEX

Aranui 52
Austral Islands 48–49
Bora Bora 35–39, 46
　Anau 38
　Faanui 38
　Lagoon 39–41
　Matira Point 38–39
　Vaitape 37–38
Bounty 10, 13, 27, 38, 41, 46, 48
Brel, Jacques 59
Cook, Captain James 9–10, 20
Fatu Hiva 62–63
Gambier Islands 46–47
Gauguin, Paul 21, 51, 58–59
Heiva 22
Hiva Oa 57–61
　Atuona 57–59
　Puamau 59–61
Huahine 28–31
　Fare 30
　Huahine Iti 31
　Maeva 30–31
Manihi 45–46
Marae 63, 64
Marquesas 51–63
Maupiti 41
Moorea 25–28, 57
　Afareaitu 26
　Cook's Bay 27–28
　Opunohu Bay 27
　Opunohu Valley 28
　Papetoai 27
　Temae 26
　Tiki Village 27
Mururoa 47
Nuku Hiva 53–56
　Anaho Bay 56
　Hakaui Valley 54
　Hatiheu Valley 55–56
　Taiohae 53–54
　Taipivai 54–55
Pearls 44

Raiatea 31–34
　Apoomau river 33
　Taputapuatea 33–34
　Uturoa 32–33
Raivavae 49
Rangiroa 42–45, 46
Rapa 49
Rimatara 48
Rurutu 48
Tahaa 34–35
Tahiti 15–23
　East coast 22–23
　Interior 23
　Taiarapu 21
　West coast 19–21
Tahuata 60
Tetiaroa 41
Tiare 34, 66
Tikehau 46
Tuamotu 42–46
Tubuai 48–49
Ua Huka 56–57
Ua Pou 57

General editor: Barbara Ender-Jones
English adaptation: Judith Farr
Editor: Christina Grisewood
Layout: Luc Malherbe
Photos: Claude Hervé-Bazin
Maps: JPM Publications

We would like to thank Tahiti Tourisme in Paris for their help
in the preparation of this guide.

Copyright © 2000 by JPM Publications SA
12 avenue William-Fraisse, 1006 Lausanne, Switzerland
E-mail: information@jpmguides.com
Web site: http://www.jpmguides.com/

All rights reserved. No part of this book may be reproduced or transmitted in any form or by any means, electronic or mechanical, including photocopying, recording or by any information storage and retrieval system without permission in writing from the publisher.

　Every care has been taken to verify the information in the guide, but the publisher cannot accept responsibility for any errors that may have occurred. If you spot an inaccuracy or a serious omission, please let us know.

Printed in Switzerland—Gessler/Sion (CTF)　　　　　　　　　　　Edition 2000–2001

FRENCH POLYNESIA

TAHITI
0 10 km
0 5 miles
PACIFIC OCEAN
TAIARAPU
Tautira
Site Archéologique
Pierres gravées
Grotte d'Anaihe
Pointe de Fareara
Mt Urau 1256 m
Mt Maitie 1073 m
Mt Orofaamu 1003 m
Mt Teoraha
Mt Ronui 1332 m
Mt Teatara 1197 m
Grotte de Vaipoiri
Toanoano
Teahupoo
Matiti
Vairao
Caverne de Maui
Teohatu
Pueu
Baie de Taravao
Taravao
Plateau de Taravao
Afaahiti
Anse Mitirapa
Port Phaeton
Papeari
Musée Gauguin
Jardin Botanique
Mataiea
Atimaono
Papara
Marae Mahaiatea
Musée du Coquillage
Grotte de Maraa
Paea
Marae Arahurahu
Marae Taata
Punaauia
Musée de Tahiti et des Iles
Lagoonarium
Taapuna
Tataa
Faaa
Papeete
Port
Pirae
Arue
Baie de Matavai
Mahina
Papenoo
Tiarei
Mahaena
Hitiaa
Faaone
Utuofai
Mt Tevaitoi 1368 m
Mt Mauru 1493 m
Mt Aramaoro 1530 m
Cascade Haamarere
Trou du Souffleur
Cascade Vaimahuta
Cascade Topatari
Cascade Puraha
Lac Vaihiria
Site Pautuna
Mt Tetufera
Pito Hiti 2110 m
Mt Orohena 2241 m
Cascade Maroto
Sentier des 1000 Sources
Mt Aorai 2066m
Mt Iviroa 1638 m
Mt Ivirairai 1696 m
Mt Marau 1493 m
Mt Te Tara O Maiao 1321 m
Fare Rau Ape
Massif du Pic Vert
Punaruu
Nairiri
Maraa

MOOREA
0 5 km
0 3 miles
Papeete
Pointe Faaupo
Temae
Lac Temae
Baie du Nuarei
Pointe Aroa
Teavaro
Vaiare
Motu Ahi
Passe Tupapaurau
Passe Teruaupu
Haumi
Umarea
Afareaitu
Ateteura
Nuupure
Marae Nuupure
Maatea
Vallée de Paoroa
Vallée de Toto
Mt Ahutaa 480m
Mt Faiurani 741m
Mt Tearai 770m
Mouaputa 830m
Teaharoa
Maharepa
Aquarium
Baie de Cook
Passe Teavarua
Paopao
Plantation d'Opuhi
Titiroa
Afareaito
Cascade
Roto Nui
Mt Tohiea 1207m
Mt Rotui 899m
Vallée d'Opunohu
Col des Trois Cocotiers
Mouaroa 830m
Baie Vaianae
Pointe Toenehua
Haapiti
Le Jardin des Roses
Passe Tareu
Baie d'Opunohu
Papetoai
Le Couloir des Raies
Vallée Terahimana
Mt Tautuapae 769m
Mouapu 762m
Passe Matauvau
Mt Parata 517m
Mt Matotea 714m
Tiki Village
Hauru
Motu Tiahura
Motu Fareone

PACIFIC OCEAN
Pointe Paharire
Motu Mute
Motu Tane
Motu Moute
Motu Haapiti
Motu Ome
Tevairoa
Pointe Taihi
Baie Hitiaa
Pointe Tereia
Apoovaio
Pointe Ofu O Rau
Baie Taimoo
Motu Tofari
Marae Fare Opu
Papoti 249 m
Motu Ahuna
Baie Faanui
Faanui
Mataihua 314 m
Marae Aehautai
Pointe Haamaire
Lagoonarium
Motu Tupe
Marae Marotet Ini
Baie Vairu
Passe Teavanui
Pointe Pahua
Marae Taianapa
Motu Tape
Pahia 661 m
Otemanu 727 m
Anau
Motu Tapu
Pointe Teaurufau
Vaitape
Pointe Araarapupu
Toopua
Baie Povaie
Baie Mataorio
Motu Piti Aau
Pointe Poofai
Pointe Paopao
Motu Toopuaiti
Pointe Raititi
Pitiuu
Motu Taurere
Pointe Matira
Aquarium
Pointe Tupititi
N
BORA BORA
0 3 km
0 2 miles